☑ **W9-AAM-293**

Like many women today, I find myself concentrating my prayer life on the demanding needs of my marriage, family, ministry, friends, our culture, and a laundry list of other things. Thanks to *A Woman's Garden of Prayer*, I am reminded that a healthy prayer life begins with cultivating the soil of my own personal relationship with Christ. I realize now, that I have permission to put my own name on my prayer list.

—BABBIE MASON, CHRISTIAN RECORDING ARTIST

A Woman's Garden of Prayer is a wonderful follow-up to *A Mother's Garden of Prayer*. Perfect for use during your daily time with the Lord, it deals with issues common in the lives of women today. Patti and Sarah's personal illustrations and gardening tips are wonderful additions, making the authors' lives transparent to the reader. You will be blessed as *A Woman's Garden of Prayer* guides you through prayer and Scripture to become more like the woman God desires you to be.

—CHRIS ADAMS, WOMEN'S ENRICHMENT MINISTRY/MINISTERS' WIVES SPECIALIST, LIFEWAY CHURCH RESOURCES

Patti Webb and Sarah Maddox have arranged Scriptures and paraphrased them into simple, beautiful prayers that address key issues in living the Christian life and in praying for others. You will find that their devotional messages offer sensitive insights to practical application of Scriptures. This book will be a blessing for women who desire to live obedient lives that are pleasing to the Lord; the prayers are those that God loves to answer, for they are according to His will, as expressed in His Word.

—KAYE JOHNS, PRAYERPOWER MINISTRIES

This is truly a beautiful book on prayer and an excellent guide to help you grow in your walk with the Lord. I especially loved the personal living illustrations and the challenges of these principles in our lives. Each page gives you the desire to love the Lord Jesus more and to draw closer to Him in prayer. Praise the Lord!

—NANCY BRAMLETT, (MRS. JOHN "BULL"), HOMEMAKER, CONFERENCE SPEAKER

What a treasure of blessings is this beautiful and insightful book written by godly, wise women for women of today. It is a combination of helpful Scriptures obviously gleaned from daily times of worship and hours of great need, stories shared from victories won in life's experiences, prayers prayed in times of trouble and rejoicing, and practical tips to encourage you as a woman to share hospitality in Jesus' sweet name. I highly recommend it to you. How it has refreshed my own life!

—JOYCE ROGERS (MRS. ADRIAN), HOMEMAKER, PASTOR'S WIFE, AUTHOR

This wonderful book gives practical and insightful guidance to the woman truly desiring intimacy with God. Sarah and Patti share their own heartfelt experiences and gently (yet firmly!) encourage the reader to deepen her own roots in this garden. Women will find inspiration and motivation to invest their time in the joy and privilege of prayer—I know I did!

—SUSIE HAWKINS (MRS. O. S.), BIBLE TEACHER, CONFERENCE SPEAKER

This charming book recounts many of the authors' experiences common to women in which God guided them to a deeper relationship to Himself through Scripture and prayer. The beauty of the scriptural applications makes the book truly a "garden" that Christian women can plant and harvest in their own lives, a treasure for those who love beauty and who love the Lord. *A Woman's Garden of Prayer* will be such a help to all of us.

—LAVERNE HUNT (MRS. T. W.) HOMEMAKER, PRAYER WARRIOR

A Woman's Garden of Prayer is an excellent book that will help women in all stages of life. It is a guide to pertinent Scripture to claim as we pray. It is a help in knowing what to pray. Sarah and Patti also encourage us with personal stories of how God has answered their prayers. This book is easy to read and to apply. Your prayer life will be enriched by the truths shared by the authors. I highly recommend it!

—ANN MIMS (MRS. GENE), HOMEMAKER, CONFERENCE SPEAKER

We will be better equipped to pray for others if we learn to pray for ourselves. This is a great tool to use to specifically and scripturally pray for all aspects of a woman's life.

—GINNY WHITEN (MRS. KEN), HOMEMAKER, WIFE OF PASTOR, IDLEWILD BAPTIST CHURCH, TAMPA, FL

CULTIVATING INTIMACY WITH GOD THROUGH PRAYER

A Woman's Garden of Prayer

BROADMAN
& HOLMAN
PUBLISHERS

Nashville, Tennessee

SARAH MADDOX & PATTI WEBB

0-8054-2498-9

Published by Broadman & Holman Publishers,
Nashville, Tennessee

Dewey Decimal Classification: 242
Subject Heading: WOMEN—PRAYER-BOOKS AND DEVOTIONS
Library of Congress Card Catalog Number: 2001

Unless otherwise stated, all Scripture quotations are from the NASB,
the New American Standard Bible, copyright © the Lockman
Foundation, 1960, 1962, 1963, 1968, 1971, 1972, 1973, 1975, 1977,
1995; used by permission. Other versions cited are used by permission;
NIV, the Holy Bible, New International Version, copyright © 1973,
1978, 1984 by International Bible Society; NRSV, the New Revised
Standard Version of the Bible, copyright © 1989 by the Division of
Christian Education of the National Council of Churches of Christ in the
United States of America, all rights reserved; TLB, The Living Bible
copyright © 1971 by Tyndale House Publishers, Wheaton, Illinois;
NKJV, the New King James Version copyright © 1979, 1980, 1982,
Thomas Nelson, Inc., Publishers; HCSB, the Holman Christian
Standard Bible, copyright © 2000 by Holman Bible Publishers;
Amplified, The Amplified Bible, copyright © 1965, 1987 by the
Zondervan Corporation and the Lockman Foundation; NLT, the Holy
Bible, New Living Translation, © 1996, used by permission of Tyndale
House Publishers, Inc., Wheaton, Illinois 60189, all rights reserved.
Scripture quotations marked KJV are from the King James Bible.

1 2 3 4 5 6 7 8 9 10   06 05 04 03 02

Sarah's Dedication

This book is dedicated to my precious mother-in-law, Lucille M. Johnson, of Clarksdale, Mississippi. For forty-two years I have observed her as she has unselfishly and lovingly shared her time, talents, and possessions with her family and friends. What a blessing she has been to my life! She is truly a "mother-in-love" to me.

Patti's Dedication

This book is dedicated to my loving mother, Naomi Suffridge Fawbush. As an octogenarian, she faithfully attends her Sunday school class and Wednesday morning Bible study each week. She inspires me to continue studying God's Word no matter my age. Tears come to my eyes when I have opportunities to sit and listen to her share about what God is teaching her. Thank you, Mother, for this godly example.

Contents

Acknowledgments

There are countless people we want to thank. Linda Dotson and Patty Hankins provided garden tips. Melana Hunt Monroe contributed an excellent illustration for the chapter on mothering.

Melanie Redd, Sarah's daughter, researched our referenced works. Vicki Crumpton encouraged us to write this second book. Janis Whipple, our editor, has lovingly guided us through the writing process. Diana Lawrence has created a beautiful design.

Prayer has been the foundation of this book. We owe a deep debt of gratitude to those who have encouraged us by their kind words and faithful prayers.

Our children— Randy and Melanie Redd, Alan and Evie Maddox, Craig and Barbara Webb, Chuck and Diane Webb—and our ten grandchildren have been a special blessing during the birthing of *A Woman's Garden of Prayer*.

But most of all we want to thank our husbands, Roland Maddox and Henry Webb. We are so blessed to have godly husbands who want us to be all God has created us to be. They have supported us emotionally and spiritually. They have listened to our agony and ecstasy as we labored to produce this manuscript. They have given so unselfishly of themselves to us—they have truly loved us as Christ loved the church.

—*Sarah Maddox and Patti Webb*

Introduction

Many Christian women are prayer warriors—great intercessors. Sometimes, however, they do not take the time to pray adequately for themselves.

Susan Lenzkes has said:

My most unselfish act may be to pray first for myself. [1]

A Woman's Garden of Prayer focuses on praying for yourself as a Christian woman. It contains Scriptures and prayers dealing with various aspects of life. We have tried to address the areas of greatest concern to women—from dealing with emotions, expectations, and endeavors, to being the wife and mother God so desires.

Elisabeth Elliot once said:

We are called to be women. The fact that I am a woman does not make me a different kind of Christian, but the fact that I am a Christian does make me a different kind of woman. For I have accepted God's idea of me, and my whole life is an offering back to Him of all that I am and all that He wants me to be. [2]

God wants us to be different—not a carbon copy of the world's idea of the beautiful woman but a unique expression of the beauty that comes from being filled with the Holy Spirit; not just a woman who prays on occasion but a prayer warrior who storms the gates of heaven for herself and for her loved ones; not a woman who demands her rights but one who lays down her rights in order to submit to the One who has a perfect will and way for her life;

not just a woman of good works but one who gives cups of cold water in the name of and for the glory of the Lord Jesus Christ; not a woman who cocoons in her home but a hospitable woman who opens her heart and her home to all whom God brings into her life; not a woman who considers her Christianity to be a private matter but a woman who spreads the sweet fragrance of the knowledge of Jesus Christ every place she goes. Yes, we are to be different, because Jesus Christ has made all the difference in our lives.

How can you and I be the kind of women God desires us to be? How can we keep from conforming to the world's mold? Only as we spend much time alone in God's presence—as we come aside each day, setting our hearts on things above, seeking His face and His will.

God calls us to come into our prayer gardens to meet with Him there. In Exodus 19:4 God reminded the people of Israel that He had brought them out of Egypt to Himself: "You yourselves have seen what I did to Egypt, and how I carried you on eagles' wings and brought you to myself" (NIV). In the garden of prayer, He draws us to Himself.

He wants us to become intimate friends of His Son, Jesus Christ. In John 15:15 Jesus said, "I have called you friends" (NIV). A friend is one in whom you can confide the deepest thoughts of your heart.

Jesus is that friend. We can tell Him our thoughts, hurts, cares, and desires. We can pray about every facet of our lives. Through prayer we can develop a sacred friendship—an intimate relationship with our Lord.

In the prayer garden, one of the best ways we can pray for ourselves is to pray Scriptures. As we pray according to His Word, our lives will be changed and our marriages strengthened; our careers can flourish and relationships blossom; the inevitable changes we encounter can turn into exciting opportunities for growth and ministry; and many of us will find the courage to begin again.

This daily time with the Lord is absolutely essential for our spiritual health. It is our lifeline to our Lord. Without it we will be powerless and unfruitful. But with it, we are ready to face the day, no matter what it may hold. For we can be assured that:

He will never leave us or forsake us.
He will guide us and guard us.
He will give us the wisdom we need and the words we need.
He will give us courage and comfort.
He will give us strength and a song to sing.
He will give us the joy of the Lord.
His peace will surround us wherever we go.
He will hear and answer as we walk in the light of His presence.

Oh, let us spend much time in the garden of prayer. "My Saviour awaits, and He opens the gates to the beautiful garden of prayer." [3]

—*Sarah Maddox*

In the Garden

I come to the garden alone,

While the dew is still on the roses;

And the voice I hear,

falling on my ear,

The Son of God discloses.

And He walks with me, and He talks with me

And He tells me I am His own,

And the joy we share as we tarry there,

None other has ever known.

—C. Austin Miles

SCRIPTURES TO PONDER

The prayer of the upright pleases him [God].
Proverbs 15:8b (NIV)

Then Jesus told his disciples . . .
that they should always pray and not give up.
Luke 18:1 (NIV)

This is the confidence we have in approaching God:
that if we ask anything according to his will, he hears us.
1 John 5:14 (NIV)

"Whatever you ask in My name, that will I do,
so that the Father may be glorified in the Son."
John 14:13

Be joyful in hope, patient in affliction, faithful in prayer.
Romans 12:12 (NIV)

And pray in the Spirit on all occasions
with all kinds of prayers and requests.
Ephesians 6:18 (NIV)

Pray continually. 1 Thessalonians 5:17 (NIV)

The prayer of a righteous man [woman] is powerful and effective.
James 5:16b (NIV)

Draw near to God and He will draw near to you.
James 4:8a

DAILY PRAYER

Oh Lord, You have told us in Your Word that the prayer of the upright pleases You. You have said that the prayer of a righteous person is powerful and effective. I have been made righteous in Your sight by the blood of the Lamb, Jesus Christ. It is only on the basis of what He has done for me at Calvary that I can come to You today. In the name of Jesus I come, asking that Your perfect will be done in every aspect of my life.

I desire to be faithful in prayer, continually seeking Your face, never giving up. May I realize anew that with You, God, nothing is impossible; but without You, I can do nothing.

As I spend time each day in my prayer garden, I want to walk with You and talk with You. I want to experience the joy that comes from spending time in Your presence. Help me daily to draw near to You. As I go from this place, may I "walk in the light of your presence" all day long (Ps. 89:15b, NIV). In Jesus' precious name I pray, *amen.*

Using This Book

Each chapter of *A Woman's Garden of Prayer* begins with Scriptures and a daily prayer pertaining to its subject. Throughout the chapter are additional Scriptures and prayers dealing with various aspects of that chapter's theme. Following the pattern of *A Mother's Garden of Prayer,* the table of contents will direct you to the specific area of your life about which you desire to pray. We suggest that you turn to the appropriate section, study the Scriptures that apply, and personalize the prayers, making them your own petitions to the Lord. After you have prayed, it is important to allow God to speak to your heart through His Word. Keep this book at your place of prayer for easy reference.

For your enjoyment and benefit, we've also included personal stories, practical applications, and garden tips.

CHAPTER ONE

Tools in My Garden

Using Expressions that Edify

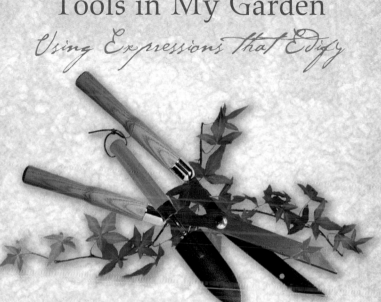

*Transformed speech results from a mind renewed
with the truth revealed through Jesus.*

—Mary A. Kassian, *Conversation Pie*

~

The words we speak are like tools in our gardens—they can be used for good or for harm. With our words we can build others up or tear them down. The woman is wise who seeks to use words that edify (build up). It is only through God's empowerment that our speech will consistently honor Him.

How delightful is a timely word! Proverbs 15:23b

The mouth of the righteous flows with wisdom. Proverbs 10:31a

The lips of the righteous know what is fitting. Proverbs 10:32a (NIV)

There is . . . a time to be silent and a time to speak.
Ecclesiastes 3:1a, 7b

He who gives an answer before he hears,
It is folly and shame to him. Proverbs 18:13

She opens her mouth in wisdom,
And the teaching of kindness is on her tongue.
Proverbs 31:26

Set a guard over my mouth, O LORD;
keep watch over the door of my lips.
Psalm 141:3 (NIV)

May the words of my mouth and the meditation of
my heart be pleasing in your sight, O LORD, my Rock
and my Redeemer. Psalm 19:14 (NIV)

Let every man be swift to hear, slow to speak,
slow to wrath. James 1:19 (KJV)

Let your speech always be with grace,
as though seasoned with salt, so that you will know
how you should respond to each person.
Colossians 4:6

Oh my Father, how I do want my words to be pleasing to You today. Set a watch over my lips, so that I will know when to speak and when to remain silent. I pray that out of my mouth will flow words of wisdom and kindness. May my speech always be gracious, "seasoned with salt." May I know how to respond to each person I encounter. May I be slow to speak and slow to become angry. Help me to listen carefully to others, not interrupting their conversations. Prompt me to speak timely, fitting words. Thank You for helping me in this important area today. In Jesus' name, *amen*.

Words as Seeds

(*Sarah*) Words are like the seeds we plant. Long after they are planted, they either bring forth good fruit or not-so-good fruit. We reap what we sow. That is God's law.

My grandfather, Rev. L. R. Riley, was a Baptist pastor for over sixty years. He was also a great sower of seeds. Behind his home in Mayfield, Kentucky, was an impressive garden covering most of the backyard. Early each morning he would hurry to the garden to begin his diligent labor of love. His thriving garden produced wonderful vegetables year after year—a bountiful tribute to my grandfather's masterful gardening skills.

But it is not that memory that lingers most in my mind. It is another kind of "seed" which Granddaddy Riley "planted" that bore the most fruit. I was privileged to witness this seed-sowing each summer of my growing-up years. We would travel from Mississippi to Kentucky to spend a week with my grandparents.

Since my grandparents did not have air-conditioning, by noon their house would become very warm. After lunch, everyone was required to take a rest. Before my rest had ended, I would hear my grandfather's heavy footsteps as he tromped from his bedroom through the house to the front door. The door squeaked as he opened it and headed for the porch swing. I can still hear the steady creak of the chains as the swing swayed back and forth, back and forth.

Soon the crunch of gravel would signal that a car had turned into the driveway. Granddaddy's feet would hit the porch floor with a thud, and I would hear him say in a loud voice, "Come on in here, boy." He would be speaking to one of the scores of young "preacher boys" who came day after day to be counseled and encouraged by my grandfather. He spent hours teaching them and admonishing them to walk in God's truth.

Only heaven will reveal all the fruits that came from those "seeds" he planted in their hearts. I praise God for the godly heritage he left to me, his only granddaughter. He showed me by his example that I am to be a planter of "seeds"—edifying words—every place I go.

We reap what we sow.
That is God's law.

Our Words as Garden Tools

Not only are our words like the seeds we plant, but they can also be compared to the tools we use in our gardens. Whether a garden is large or small, simple or ornate, certain tools are needed to cultivate it and keep it looking beautiful. These tools, however, can be used for good, or they can be misused.

Our words, like tools, can be used for good, or they can do great harm. It is essential that we learn to use our words wisely.

Death and life are in the power of the tongue.

Garden Shears

DON'T USE CUTTING, HARSH WORDS

Let the words of my mouth and the meditation of my heart
Be acceptable in Your sight, O LORD, my rock and my Redeemer.
Psalm 19:14

A gentle answer turns away wrath,
But a harsh word stirs up anger. Proverbs 15:1

She opens her mouth in wisdom,
And the teaching of kindness is on her tongue. Proverbs 31:26

Death and life are in the power of the tongue. Proverbs 18:21a

Reckless words pierce like a sword, but the tongue of the wise brings healing. Truthful lips endure forever, but a lying tongue lasts only a moment. Proverbs 12:18–19 (NIV)

He who guards his lips guards his life, but he who speaks rashly will come to ruin. Proverbs 13:3 (NIV)

See also Psalm 52:4; Proverbs 10:32

~

PRAYER

Dear Father, when I am upset or do not like someone, it is so easy to let cutting words roll off my tongue. Sometimes these piercing words come so easily. When that happens, I know that my heart is not right toward You. I realize that when I use cutting words it is because I want to hurt that person. Please forgive me.

I desire to speak words that heal; I desire to guard my lips. I want to speak with wisdom. Holy Spirit, before I speak, would You make me aware of the words that are about to come off my tongue. May the words of my mouth and the meditations of my heart be acceptable in Your sight today. In Jesus' name, *amen.*

He who covers a transgression seeks love, but he who repeats a matter separates intimate friends.

Shovel

DON'T SHOVEL OUT DIRT ABOUT OTHERS (GOSSIP)

A perverse man spreads strife,
And a slanderer separates intimate friends. Proverbs 16:28

He who conceals a transgression seeks love,
But he who repeats a matter separates intimate friends. Proverbs 17:9

He who spreads slander is a fool. Proverbs 10:18b

The words of a talebearer are like tasty trifles,
And they go down into the inmost body. Proverbs 18:8 (NKJV)

He who goes about as a slanderer reveals secrets,
Therefore do not associate with a gossip. Proverbs 20:19

Without wood a fire goes out;
without gossip a quarrel dies down. Proverbs 26:20 (NIV)

See also Proverbs 17:1

PRAYER

Father, it is so easy for me to want to repeat words about this matter (or person) that should not be repeated. I do not want to be a perverse woman who spreads strife and slander. Your Word says that when I gossip about a person, it hurts him or her like a wound in the inmost body. I know that gossip separates friends. I know also, Father, that when I do not repeat a matter, it dies down. Thank You for that assurance. Help me not to gossip or to associate with those who gossip. Give me strength to follow Your teachings in this matter. In Jesus' name, *amen.*

Rake

DON'T RAKE OTHERS "OVER THE COALS"

There is one who speaks rashly like the thrusts of a sword,
But the tongue of the wise brings healing. Proverbs 12:18

Death and life are in the power of the tongue. Proverbs 18:21a

Better to dwell in the wilderness, than with a contentious
and an angry woman. Proverbs 21:19 (KJV)

But no man can tame the tongue. It is a restless evil, full of deadly
poison. With the tongue we praise our Lord and Father, and with it
we curse men, who have been made in God's likeness. Out of the same
mouth come praise and cursing. My brothers, this should not be.
James 3:8–10 (NIV)

~

PRAYER

Dear heavenly Father, please help me today. I have been rash in my speaking. I have been a contentious and angry woman. I have raked _____ "over the coals," and I feel terrible about it. Please forgive me, Lord. I realize that death and life are in the power of the tongue. I acknowledge that my speaking rashly is like the thrust of a sword. I know I have done wrong. I want to change. Only You can change me, Lord. In my own strength I cannot tame my tongue. It is a "restless evil, full of deadly poison."

So today, oh Lord, I ask that You reveal to me any unconfessed sin in my heart that is causing me to sin with my mouth. "For the mouth speaks out of that which fills the heart" (Matt. 12:34b). I do confess this sin. Thank You for the changes You will work in my heart and life. In Jesus' name, *amen.*

... put devious speech far from you.

Hoe

DON'T HOE ROWS OF DECEIT AND FALSEHOOD

Lying lips are an abomination to the LORD. Proverbs 12:22a

The LORD hates ... a false witness who utters lies. Proverbs 6:16a, 19a

Be not a witness against thy neighbour without cause; and deceive not with thy lips. Proverbs 24:28 (KJV)

Put away from you a deceitful mouth,
And put devious speech far from you. Proverbs 4:24

Whoever would love life and see good days must keep his tongue from evil and his lips from deceitful speech. 1 Peter 3:10 (NIV)

PRAYER

Oh God, here I am again. I always want to speak the truth, but it seems so hard to do. You have told me that I must put away from me a deceitful mouth and devious lips. Help me not to be deceitful in small or large matters today. May I never be a false witness who utters lies. Help me to remember that there are no "white lies" in Your sight. I am looking to You for Your empowerment to keep my tongue from evil and my lips from deceitful speech. Thank You, oh God. I need You. In Jesus' name, *amen.*

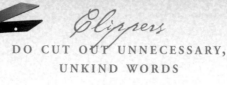

Clippers

DO CUT OUT UNNECESSARY, UNKIND WORDS

Set a guard over my mouth, O LORD;
keep watch over the door of my lips. Psalm 141:3 (NIV)

Keep your tongue from evil
and your lips from speaking lies. Psalm 34:13 (NIV)

He who guards his mouth and his tongue,
Guards his soul from troubles. Proverbs 21:23

A fool uttereth all his mind: but a wise man keepeth it
in till afterwards. Proverbs 29:11 (KJV)

Do not repay evil with evil or insult with insult, but with blessing,
because to this you were called so that you may inherit a blessing.
1 Peter 3:9 (NIV)

Everyone must be quick to hear, slow to speak and slow to anger.
James 1:19

See also Proverbs 13:3

~

PRAYER

Dearest Lord, I need Your help in guarding my mouth. Only You can enable me to stay out of trouble. I want to keep my tongue from evil and my lips from speaking lies. I want to be quick to hear and slow to speak. I do not want to return insult for insult but rather, when I am insulted, to return blessings.

Lord, I know I cannot possibly fulfill these desires in my own strength. Therefore, I ask for the restraining power of the Holy Spirit to guard my lips all day long. In Jesus' name, *amen.*

Sprinkler

DO SPLASH JOY ON EVERYONE YOU MEET

A man has joy by the answer of his mouth,
And a word spoken in due season, how good it is! Proverbs 15:23 (NKJV)

Anxiety in the heart of man causes depression,
But a good word makes it glad. Proverbs 12:25 (NKJV)

Pleasant words are as an honeycomb, sweet to the soul,
and health to the bones. Proverbs 16:24 (KJV)

If anyone speaks, he should do it as one speaking
the very words of God. 1 Peter 4:11 (NIV)

Let no unwholesome word proceed from your mouth, but only such
a word as is good for edification according to the need of the moment,
so that it may give grace to those who hear. Ephesians 4:29

~

PRAYER

Dear Father in heaven, I want to splash joy on everyone today! Please help me to do just that! So many people are hurting and need a fitting word of encouragement or comfort. May I speak Your words. May no unwholesome word proceed from my mouth but only those words that will build up others, according to their needs. I desire that my words be pleasant like a honeycomb, "sweet to the soul" of the person who hears them. May they be loving, healing words. I pray that many people will be made glad because of my words today. This I pray in the joyful name of Jesus, *amen.*

Practical Tip

(*Sarah*) In my brother's Bible I found a folded sheet of notebook paper with this advice, which is certainly applicable today. My brother wrote:

Always ask these questions before you speak:
Is it true? Is it kind? Is it necessary?

My brother, Joe Thomas Odle, lived only twenty years. In October of his junior year at Mississippi College, it was discovered that he had Hodgkins disease. Three months later, on January 31, 1955, Joe went to be with the Lord. With his untimely death, this young ministerial student preached a "sermon" to all who knew him. His "text" was the passage underlined in red in his personal Bible: Philippians 1:20b–21: "So now also Christ shall be magnified in my body, whether it be by life, or by death. For to me to live is Christ, and to die is gain" (KJV). For Joe, to die was gain. We who were left behind must live for Christ.

Garden Tip

Garden tools can get rusty and useless so quickly. To prevent this, fill a bucket with sand. Add a little lubricating oil (such as WD40) to the sand. When you finish using your clippers, trowels, and other tools, store them in the bucket of sand. The abrasive nature of the sand will clean off any leftover dirt, and the oil will lubricate them.

CHAPTER TWO

Weeding and Feeding
Handling My Emotions

*The problem is not that we have emotions.
The challenge is to let the Spirit of God sanctify us in the realm of
our emotions so they can be expressed in godly ways.*
—*Nancy DeMoss, Lies Women Believe*

~

Emotions, both positive and negative, can rule women's lives. Godly women recognize when destructive emotions reign. They run to God, asking for His help in "digging up" the negative emotions. They then begin to "plant" the emotions that will enable them to reflect His love and grace.

everything we need for life . . .

To those who through the righteousness of our God and Savior
Jesus Christ have received a faith as precious as ours . . . His divine
power has given us everything we need for life and godliness through
our knowledge of him who called us by his own glory and goodness.
Through these he has given us his very great and precious promises,
so that through them you may participate in the divine nature
and escape the corruption in the world caused by evil desires.

2 Peter 1:1b, 3–4 (NIV)

*he has given us
very great and
precious promises...*

~

DAILY PRAYER

Dear God, thank You that Your divine power has given me everything I need to become a godly woman—a woman who pleases You.
I praise You that as I believe and obey Your Word, I will become more
like You. As I learn more about You, You will give me the power and
knowledge to escape the corruption in the world caused by evil
desires. In Your precious name, *amen.*

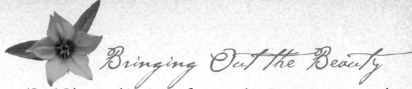

Bringing Out the Beauty

(*Patti*) I love working in my flower garden. I may emerge covered with dirt, feeling hot and sweaty, tired and exhausted, but I am revived in my soul. I find myself wandering along the newly pruned flower beds, looking at the freshly turned soil. I relish the new growth, the profusion of colorful blooms, and various hues of greenery that appear after pruning. As soon as someone appears, I call, "Come see my garden."

However, at other times I do not want anyone to see my garden. It usually happens in August, our dry month in Nashville. Unless I have worked to weed and prune in the earlier months, I cannot keep up with the many weeds and unruly flowers. If I have not looked for those weeds hidden under the blooms of May, June, and July, then August will produce weeds that choke out the beauty of my garden.

A similar thing happens with my emotions. If I do not constantly ask God to weed out my negative emotions, when the "dry spells" come, such as fatigue, illness, daily pressures, or crises, those destructive thoughts take over. Without my realizing it, the "weeds" choke out the beauty that God has planted in my life.

Weeding is a part of gardening. Although necessary, it is to me and most gardeners I know, a most unpleasant task. I can take out the unwanted growth one day. The next morning I find new weeds. It takes constant attention to keep weeds under control.

In my daily life, new or old destructive emotions can pop up. I need to let God remove them when they are small and not out of control.

Destructive Emotions
EMOTIONS WE NEED TO WEED OUT OF OUR LIVES

Anxiety

I sought the LORD, and he answered me;
he delivered me from all my fears. Psalm 34:4 (NIV)

Do not fret because of evil men or be envious of those who do wrong;
for like the grass they will soon wither, like green plants
they will soon die away. . . . Do not fret—it leads only to evil.
Psalm 37:1–2, 8 (NIV)

Do not be anxious about anything, but in everything, by prayer and
petition, with thanksgiving, present your requests to God. And the
peace of God, which transcends all understanding, will guard your
hearts and your minds in Christ Jesus. Philippians 4:6–7 (NIV)

Be self-controlled and alert. Your enemy the devil prowls around like
a roaring lion looking for someone to devour. 1 Peter 5:8 (NIV)

PRAYER

Oh Father, I am so anxious today because of _____.
You have told me not to be anxious and fretful. Please forgive me. I
desire the peace that only You can give when everything around me
is collapsing. You are the One who will deliver me from this emotional upheaval. I thank You ahead of time that You are going to
work in me to change my emotions.

I now commit every detail of my emotional state to You in earnest and thankful prayer. (*List details.*) I ask for Your peace which will guard my heart and mind in Christ Jesus. Help me to be self-controlled and alert, so that I will not give in to the devil's schemes. In Jesus' name, *amen.*

. . . like the grass they will soon wither, like green plants they will soon die away . . . Fear

Give thanks to the Lord, for he is good; his love endures forever. The LORD is with me; I will not be afraid. What can man do to me? The LORD is with me; he is my helper. I will look in triumph on my enemies. It is better to take refuge in the LORD than to trust in man.
Psalm 118:1, 6–8 (NIV)

When I am afraid, I will put my trust in You. In God, whose word I praise, In God I have put my trust; I shall not be afraid. What can mere man do to me? Psalm 56:3–4

"Be strong and courageous. Do not be afraid or terrified because of them, for the LORD your God goes with you; he will never leave you nor forsake you." Deuteronomy 31:6 (NIV)

He who dwells in the shelter of the Most High will abide in the shadow of the Almighty. I will say to the LORD, "My refuge and my fortress, My God, in whom I trust!" . . . and under His wings you may seek refuge; His faithfulness is a shield and bulwark. You will not be afraid of the terror by night. Psalm 91:1–2, 4b, 5a

PRAYER

Father, You are so good. Thank You that Your love endures forever. You have told me to be strong and courageous, and to put my trust in You. As my refuge and fortress, I know I can find shelter under Your protective wings. That is what I desire.

Right now I am full of fear about _____. I am terrified because of _____. I know it is better to take refuge in You than to believe what man says or to fear what man can do to me. I am afraid, Father, but I am choosing to trust in You. I do not want to allow this destructive emotion to rule my life. I believe; help my unbelief. In Jesus' name, *amen*.

Get rid of all bitterness, rage and anger, brawling and slander, along with every form of malice.

Anger

"In your anger do not sin": Do not let the sun go down while you are still angry, and do not give the devil a foothold. . . . Get rid of all bitterness, rage and anger, brawling and slander, along with every form of malice. Be kind and compassionate to one another, forgiving each other, just as in Christ God forgave you.

Ephesians 4:26–27, 31–32 (NIV)

My dear brothers, take note of this: Everyone should be quick to listen, slow to speak and slow to become angry, for man's anger does not bring about the righteous life that God desires. James 1:19–20 (NIV)

A quick-tempered man acts foolishly, and a man of evil devices is hated. . . . He who is slow to anger has great understanding, But he who is quick-tempered exalts folly. Proverbs 14:17, 29

He who is slow to anger is better than the mighty, and he who rules his spirit than he who takes a city. Proverbs 16:32 (NKJV)

The beginning of strife is like letting out water, So abandon the quarrel before it breaks out. Proverbs 17:14

Do not be eager in your heart to be angry, For anger resides in the bosom of fools. Ecclesiastes 7:9

See also Proverbs 29:22 (NIV); Colossians 3:5–8

~

PRAYER

Dear God, I am so angry about _____. I am close to saying or doing something foolish that will not honor You. This anger I feel is not a righteous anger. You have said that when I am angry, I am a fool. I do not want to be a fool. I do not want to bury this anger and let it reside in my bosom. Teach me how to handle this potentially destructive emotion. It is destroying me.

May I see this situation through Your eyes. I desire to obey You. I do not want to start an argument. I ask that You help me control my spirit. I want my thoughts to be godly and my actions to please You. In Jesus' name, *amen.*

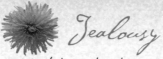

Jealousy

Wrath is cruel and anger a torrent,
But who is able to stand before jealousy? Proverbs 27:4 (NKJV)

Who is wise and understanding among you? Let him show by good
conduct that his works are done in the meekness of wisdom. But if you
have bitter envy and self-seeking in your hearts, do not boast and lie
against the truth. This wisdom does not descend from above, but is
earthly, sensual, demonic. For where envy and self-seeking exist,
confusion and every evil thing are there. James 3:13–16 (NKJV)

Rejoice with those who rejoice, and weep with those who weep.
Romans 12:15

Do nothing from selfishness or empty conceit, but with humility
of mind let each of you regard one another as more important
than yourselves; do not merely look out for your own personal interests,
but also for the interests of others. Philippians 2:3–4

PRAYER

Father, I confess that I am jealous about _____. You are clear in Your
Word that when I am jealous, I am not having godly thoughts. I am selfish and envious right now and do not want to look out for the interest
of _____. Please forgive me. I agree with You that these destructive feelings are earthly, sensual, and demonic. I do not want to feel this way. I
humble myself before You; I desire to regard _____ as more important
than myself. Please help me to love this person and to rejoice in what is
happening to her. Your power will enable me to change my thoughts
from jealous thoughts to godly thoughts. In Jesus' name, *amen.*

Bitterness

Let all bitterness, wrath, anger, clamor, and evil speaking be put away from you, with all malice. Ephesians 4:31 (NKJV)

See to it that no one comes short of the grace of God; that no root of bitterness springing up causes trouble, and by it many be defiled. Hebrews 12:15

See also Proverbs 14:10

~

PRAYER

Dear God, I am having trouble with bitterness about ____. My heart is full of bitterness, and it is affecting those around me. I confess this sin and choose to put it away from me. Please forgive me. In Jesus' name, *amen.*

Losing Control

The evil deeds of a wicked man ensnare him; the cords of his sin hold him fast. He will die for lack of discipline, led astray by his own great folly. Proverbs 5:22–23 (NIV)

But everyone must be quick to hear, slow to speak and slow to anger; for the anger of man does not achieve the righteousness of God. James 1:19b–20

He who is slow to anger is better than the mighty, And he who rules his spirit, than he who captures a city. Proverbs 16:32

Do you see a man who speaks in haste? There is more hope for a fool than for him. Proverbs 29:20 (NIV)

See also Proverbs 29:11

PRAYER

Oh my Father, I have "blown" it again. I have lost my temper and caused great trouble. Please forgive me. I do not want to be led astray by my own folly. I know that "he that is slow to anger is better than the mighty." I want to be "slow to speak and slow to anger." I know that my anger does not achieve Your righteousness. But Lord, I cannot handle my anger in my own strength. Please work in me so that I will become a woman who controls her spirit—a wise woman. Thank You for Your help in this matter. In Jesus' precious name, *amen.*

Guilt, Shame

Rather, we have renounced secret and shameful ways; we do not use deception, nor do we distort the word of God. 2 Corinthians 4:2 (NIV)

Have mercy on me, O God, according to your unfailing love; according to your great compassion blot out my transgressions. Wash away all my iniquity and cleanse me from my sin. Psalm 51:1–2 (NIV)

If we confess our sins, He is faithful and just to forgive us our sins and to cleanse us from all unrighteousness. 1 John 1:9 (NKJV)

See also John 16:8

~

PRAYER

Oh Lord, I am filled with guilt and shame. I come to You renouncing _____. (*List any secret or shameful ways.*) Please have mercy on me, oh God, according to Your unfailing love and great compassion. I now confess my sins. (*Name them, as God brings them to your mind.*) Please forgive me and cleanse me from all unrighteousness. I want to be pure and holy. In Jesus' name, *amen.*

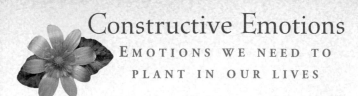

Constructive Emotions
EMOTIONS WE NEED TO
PLANT IN OUR LIVES

Self-Control

Like a city that is broken into and without walls
Is a man who has no control over his spirit. Proverbs 25:28

See also 1 Peter 5:8 (NIV)

Meekness

The meek also shall increase their joy in the LORD. Isaiah 29:19a (KJV)

See also Psalm 37:11; Psalm 149:4; Matthew 3:4; 1 Peter 3:4

Quiet Spirit

Do not let your adornment be merely outward —arranging the hair,
wearing gold, or putting on fine apparel —rather let it be the hidden
person of the heart, with the incorruptible beauty of a gentle and
quiet spirit, which is very precious in the sight of God.
1 Peter 3:3–4 (NKJV)

See also 1 Thessalonians 2:7 (NKJV); 1 Timothy 3:3 (NKJV);
2 Timothy 2:24 (NKJV); Titus 3:2 (NKJV); James 3:17 (NKJV)

Love

"A new command I give you: Love one another. As I have loved you,
so you must love one another." John 13:34 (NIV)

See also Matthew 5:44; Romans 12:9 (NIV); Romans 13:10;
1 Corinthians 13; 1 Corinthians 16:14; 1 Peter 1:22 (NIV)

Joy

You have made known to me the path of life;
you will fill me with joy in your presence. Psalm 16:11 (NIV)

See also Jeremiah 15:16 (NKJV); Psalm 30:5b; Habakkuk 3:18 (NKJV);
Isaiah 61:10a (NKJV); Psalm 19:8a (NIV)

Peace

You will keep him in perfect peace, whose mind is stayed on You,
Because he trusts in You. Isaiah 26:3 (NKJV)

See also Proverbs 14:30 (NIV); Psalm 119:165 (NIV); Isaiah 32:17 (NIV);
Isaiah 48:18 (NIV); John 14:27; Romans 8:6b; Philippians 4:6–7

Patience

Love is patient, love is kind. It does not envy, it does not boast,
it is not proud. 1 Corinthians 13:4 (NIV)

Be patient with everyone. 1 Thessalonians 5:14b (NIV)

See also Proverbs 15:18; 2 Corinthians 6:3–6; Galatians 5:22

~
PRAYER

Oh my Abba Father, I desire to be a woman who walks in the Spirit and exemplifies the fruit of the Spirit in my everyday life. I know that I am to exercise self-control and display a meek and quiet spirit. I know that my life is to be filled with love and joy. I need to be patient and long-suffering with the difficult people in my life. I need to be gentle and kind. I desire to manifest Your peace in every situation. But this is so hard, Lord. In certain of these areas I am so weak. Please help me today to work on _____. (*See list on previous page with accompanying Scriptures.*) As I apply Your words to my life, may these godly character-istics be developed in me. Thank You, dear Lord. In Jesus' name, *amen.*

Practical Tip

(*Patti*) As women, dealing with our unhealthy emotions is some-times difficult. I use the following acrostic from *MasterLife* when I find my emotional responses do not measure up to God's standard. God has shown me how to turn my destructive emotions into godly emotions. He is the One who shows me how to weed out destructive emotions.

ACTION PLAN[1]

A Acknowledge your emotions. (*Do not deny how you feel. Tell God the exact emotion you are experiencing.*)

C Consider why you have it. (*Think about the underlying cause of this destructive emotion. Does it stem from a physical problem, a relationship problem, faulty thinking, etc.?*)

T Thank God that He will help you master it. *(Choose to thank God that He is going to handle your emotions.)*

I Identify the biblical response to it. *(Go to God's Word to find the appropriate scriptural response for you in this situation.)*

O Obey the Holy Spirit's leading. *(Do what God's Word tells you to do.)*

N Nurture the appropriate fruit of the Spirit. (Gal. 5:22–23) *(Evaluate your responses according to these godly characteristics.)*

If it is your desire to be a consistent, spiritually mature Christian woman, ask the Lord to reveal in your life the destructive emotions that need to be "weeded out" and the constructive emotions that need to be "planted."

> *Sow for yourselves righteousness; reap in mercy;*
> *Break up your fallow ground, for it is time to seek the LORD;*
> *Till He comes and rains righteousness on you.*
> Hosea 10:12 *(NKJV)*

Garden Tip

When you plant flowers in the backyard that can be viewed from your windows, plant white flowers. They will reflect the moonlight and make your yard glow in the dark.

CHAPTER THREE

A Perennial Challenge

Dealing with Expectations

We can learn contentment whether we are single or married, with career or without career. Contentment from God's perspective cuts out the "superwoman syndrome" and brings in the "satisfied-woman syndrome."
—L. Jane Mohline, A Woman of Excellence

*U*nmet expectations can steal our joy, peace, and contentment if they are not put in proper perspective. Disappointments can arise when a person does not live up to what we had expected. Seeing others through God's eyes and giving our expectations to Him must become a way of life. As we depend on the Lord in every situation, we can learn to be content.

My soul, wait silently for God alone,
For my expectation is from Him. Psalm 62:5 (NKJV)

In the morning, O LORD, . . . I lay my requests before you
and wait in expectation. Psalm 5:3 (NIV)

Our adequacy [sufficiency] is from God. 2 Corinthians 3:5b

The LORD's lovingkindnesses indeed never cease,
For His compassions never fail. They are new every morning;
Great is Your faithfulness. Lamentations 3:22–23

DAILY PRAYER

Oh dear God, my soul waits upon You today. I know that my expectations are to be in You. I affirm that my sufficiency is from You and You alone. May I not attempt to live out this day in my own strength but in the strength that You supply. I praise You for Your love for me and Your faithfulness to me. As I now lay before You my requests, I will wait in expectation for Your answers. (*Name your requests at this time.*) In Jesus' holy name, *amen.*

Turning Over Expectations

(*Sarah*) The phone rang on Sunday night. It was our weekly call from my parents, Joe and Mabel Odle. After a few moments of exchanging the latest family tidbits, Daddy informed us that he would be coming to Memphis on Thursday. It was summer and light enough for me to see my front yard lying barren in the twilight.

Oh dear, I thought to myself. *What will Daddy think of our yard? The Odles' yard looks like a golf course, and ours more like a baseball field. What can I do?*

As I hung up the phone, I realized that "bugging" Roland about the yard was not the thing to do! He had worked diligently trying to get grass to grow under our many oak trees, planting rye grass, Kentucky bluegrass, and zoysia. He had fertilized and watered, but to no avail. Those bare spots stood glaringly for all to see.

Remembering a principle I had recently heard, I got on my knees the next morning to give the situation to the Lord. You see, in a Christian marriage seminar we had been challenged to give our expectations of our mates to God, trusting Him with the results. So that Monday morning I gave my expectations of having a pretty yard by Thursday to the Lord and got up from my knees, leaving the results in His hands.

On Tuesday our next-door neighbor called unexpectedly. I would never have dreamed what his next words would be. He told me that he was digging up half of his backyard for a garden and wondered if I would like to have the sod to cover the bald spots in my front yard.

"Of course I would! How wonderful!" I exclaimed. How excited I was to know that my yard would look good for Daddy's coming. But even more exciting was the fact that when I gave my expectations to the Lord, He answered in a way I could never have thought of, much less expected. In my mind there was just no way the yard could look good by Thursday, but God had it all planned out. He just wanted me to give my expectations to Him. As an added blessing, Daddy loved hearing about the way our yard got "prettied up" for his coming.

I have never forgotten the lesson God taught me that week: when I give my expectations of others to God, He will "do exceedingly abundantly above all that we ask or think" (Eph. 3:20, NKJV). Praise His name!

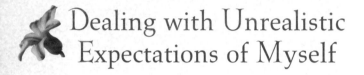

Dealing with Unrealistic Expectations of Myself

Why are you downcast, O my soul? . . . Put your hope in God.
Psalm 42:11 (NIV)

I can do all things through Him [Christ] who strengthens me.
Philippians 4:13

He guides me in paths of righteousness for his name's sake.
Psalm 23:3b (NIV)

Be filled with the Spirit. Ephesians 5:18b (NIV)

So I say, live by the Spirit, and you will not gratify the desires of the sinful nature. Galatians 5:16 (NIV)

Finally, be strong in the Lord and in his mighty power.
Ephesians 6:10 (NIV)

PRAYER

Oh Father, I am so disappointed with myself today. I expected so much more of me. I know it is not Your will for me to have unrealistic expectations of myself. You have not asked me to live up to the standard of perfection. Jesus was the only One who was perfect. I am depending too much on my own wisdom and strength instead of looking to You.

Please reveal to me what You expect from me. May I seek Your will and Your ways for my life. May I walk in the paths You have laid out for me—the paths of righteousness. I know I can do all the things You expect of me through the strength of the One who lives within me—Jesus Christ.

Please fill me with Your Holy Spirit, so that I will not seek to fulfill the desires of my sinful nature. I want to be strong in the Lord and in Your mighty power. In Jesus' name, *amen.*

... regard no one from a worldly point of view.

Dealing with Unmet Expectations of Others

For the LORD searches all hearts, and understands every intent of the thoughts. 1 Chronicles 28:9b

So from now on we regard no one from a worldly point of view. 2 Corinthians 5:16 (NIV)

*You turn things around! Shall the potter be considered as equal
with the clay, that what is made would say to its maker,
"He did not make me"; or what is formed say to him who formed it,
"He has no understanding"? Isaiah 29:16*

If any of you lacks wisdom, he should ask God. James 1:5 (NIV)

*"For You [God] and You only know the hearts of all the children of men."
1 Kings 8:39 (Amplified)*

*"For the Lord sees not as man sees . . . The Lord looks on the heart."
1 Samuel 16:7b (Amplified)*

See also John 14:20–21 (HCSB); Proverbs 20:5 (NIV)

~

PRAYER

Father, thank You that You search and know my heart and the
heart of _____ . Right now I disagree with her actions. I confess
to You that I have unrealistic expectations. Oh God, change my heart
so that instead of looking at her from a worldly point of view, I can
see her through Your eyes.

Father, sometimes I think I am the potter who can reshape this person. I want to change my heart and mind concerning _____.
Please enable me to allow her to be the woman You made her to be,
without imposing my expectations on her. Forgive me for trying to
be in charge of her life.

As I deal with her, I need Your wisdom and perspective. You alone
know her heart. I praise You that Your wisdom will guide me to see
her as You see her. In Jesus' name, *amen.*

Learning to Be Content

I have learned the secret of being content
in any and every situation. Philippians 4:12 (NIV)

But godliness with contentment is great gain. 1 Timothy 6:6 (NIV)

Give thanks in all circumstances, for this is God's will for you
in Christ Jesus. 1 Thessalonians 5:18 (NIV)

And my God will meet all your needs according to his glorious riches
in Christ Jesus. Philippians 4:19 (NIV)

And be content with what you have, because God has said,
"Never will I leave you; never will I forsake you." Hebrews 13:5b (NIV)

See also 2 Corinthians 3:5

~

PRAYER

Dear heavenly Father, today I am filled with discontent. I seem to be dwelling on my unmet expectations. I know this is not Your will for me—You want me to learn to be content in any and every situation. This is so hard for me, Lord. I really need Your help in this matter. Please empower and enable me to learn to be content, no matter the circumstances.

May I concentrate on what I have, not on what I lack. May I be flooded with an attitude of gratitude. Help me to remember that as a Christian woman, all Your glorious riches in Christ Jesus are available to supply my needs. You, O God, are Jehovah Shammah—You are always with me. You will never leave me or forsake me. Help me to walk in the light of these truths. In Jesus' name, *amen*.

Trusting in God

May your unfailing love rest upon us, O Lord,
even as we put our hope in you. Psalm 33:22 (NIV)

For you have been my hope, O Sovereign Lord,
my confidence since my youth. Psalm 71:5 (NIV)

This I recall to my mind, therefore I have hope. The Lord's loving-
kindnesses indeed never cease, for His compassions never fail. They are
new every morning; great is Your faithfulness. Lamentations 3:21–23

My soul, wait silently for God alone, for my expectation is from Him.
Psalm 62:5 (NKJV)

Trust in the Lord with all your heart. Proverbs 3:5a

I wait for the Lord, . . . and in his word I put my hope. Psalm 130:5 (NIV)

May the God of hope fill you with all joy and peace as you trust in him,
so that you may overflow with hope by the power of the Holy Spirit.
Romans 15:13 (NIV)

See also Psalm 42:11

PRAYER

Dearest Lord, please forgive me for looking to _____ to meet my expectations. You are the One I should be looking to; my expectation is to be from You. You are my hope. You love me with an unfailing love. Your loving-kindness is new every morning. Your compassions never fail. Great is Thy faithfulness.

Oh Father, I want to trust in You with all my heart. Please enable me to wait for You to work in this situation. Fill me with joy and peace as I put my trust in You, so that I may overflow with hope by the power of Your Holy Spirit. Help me to remember that because You are Jehovah Jireh, my provider, You are more than enough for me. In Your blessed name I pray, *amen.*

*And they that know thy name will put their trust in thee:
for thou, LORD, hast not forsaken them that seek thee.
Psalm 9:10 (KJV)*

Names of God

El Roi: The God Who Sees

El Shaddai: The All-Sufficient One

Adonai: LORD, Master

Jehovah Jireh: The LORD Will Provide

Jehovah Raah: The LORD, My Shepherd

Jehovah Shammah: The LORD Is There

Practical Tip

For a week, try giving all your expectations of someone to God. Then sit back and watch what God will do!

Garden Tip

A wisteria must experience some stress to bloom. If this plant is grown in an area where that natural stress does not occur, it will not bloom. The gardener can put artificial "stress" on the trunk, and it will give beautiful flowers. The best way to let the plant experience stress is by hitting it hard three times with a baseball bat. It will then "bloom up a storm."

CHAPTER FOUR

Welcome to My Garden

Encircling Others

*All the charm and beauty a woman
may have amounts to nothing if her ambitions are self-centered.
But if she reflects her Creator and assumes the posture of a graceful
servant, she cannot help but command high respect and favor.*

—Jeanne Hendricks, *Promises, Promises*

God brings many people into the gardens of our lives. He wants us to open our hearts to those who come our way just as the flowers open up to the sunshine. Whether it's by sharing joyfully with others, being hospitable, learning to love one who is different, or giving the gift of encouragement, each of us needs to encircle those whom God sends into our paths.

But serve one another through love. Galatians 5:13b (HCSB)

DAILY PRAYER

Holy Father, help me to serve everyone I encounter in a loving way. In Jesus' name, *amen.*

A Tea Party

(*Patti*) To me there is nothing more relaxing than friends and a tea tray. Sometimes I use a silver tray with fine china, white linen napkins, a beautiful flower from my garden nestled in a tiny vase, and a favorite teapot with loose tea brewing. At other times simple mugs and tea bags will suffice. Just being with a friend gives me great pleasure, whether sitting in the garden, on the patio, or inside by a warm fire. This is what it means to be hospitable—focusing on the people, not the surroundings or the accoutrements. Simply enjoying the moment to lavish attention on others—the joy of sharing. Friendship, not the surroundings, enhances your time together. For me it is a tea tray. For others it might be a game of Scrabble. Each person can find something special to share with friends.

There was a time when I did not have this outlook on hospitality. I misunderstood the word *hospitable.* I thought I had to have everything perfect in my home before people were invited over. I made my poor family miserable as we prepared for guests. No more. Now people are invited to my home for friendship and hospitality, not to view a perfect house or eat perfect refreshments. This has been liberating.

... he who refreshes others will himself be refreshed.

Sharing Joyfully

(*Sarah*) My mother-in-law, Lucille Johnson, is one of the most merciful and loving women I have ever known. What an ideal mother-in-love she has been for these forty years I have been married to her son. She has always seemed to find such joy in sharing with her family and friends.

A few years ago when Lucille moved from her home into an apartment, she no longer had room for some of her prized possessions. One of these was the set of good china she had used all through her marriage to Roland's dad. I asked her if we might have the joy of using it in our home. She was thrilled for me to have it. Now each time I serve a meal on this beautiful, green-bordered, floral china, I am reminded of the wonderful lady who for so many years has joyfully shared with others.

> *One man gives freely, yet gains even more;*
> *another withholds unduly, but comes to poverty.*
> *A generous man will prosper; he who refreshes others*
> *will himself be refreshed. Proverbs 11:24–25 (NIV)*

> *"And whoever gives just a cup of cold water to one of these little ones*
> *because he is a disciple —I assure you: He will never lose his reward!"*
> *Matthew 10:42 (HCSB)*

"Give, and it will be given to you; a good measure, pressed down, shaken together, and running over will be poured into your lap. For with the measure that you use, it will be measured back to you."
Luke 6:38 (HCSB)

Share with the saints in their needs; pursue hospitality. Bless those who persecute you; bless and do not curse. Rejoice with those who rejoice; weep with those who weep.
Romans 12:13–15 (HCSB)

Let brotherly love continue. Don't neglect to show hospitality, for by doing this some have welcomed angels as guests without knowing it.
Hebrews 13:1–2 (HCSB)

~

PRAYER

Oh Father, help me to realize the importance of giving to others. You have said that with the measure I use in my giving, it will be measured back to me. I know that when I give freely, I will gain even more. When I splash water on others, I will be watered myself. Help me today to look for opportunities to give cups of cold water in Your name.

May I continually show brotherly love. May I realize that as I show hospitality to those in my world, without even knowing it, I could be welcoming angels as guests. Help me to share joyfully with the saints who are in need. Please enable me to bless those who persecute me, rejoice with those who rejoice, and weep with those who weep. In Jesus' precious name I pray, *amen*.

Practicing Hospitality

(*Patti*) The antique Spode china cup and saucer are pieces I reach for often. The cup's gently curving lip and fine detailed pattern warm my heart. This cup and saucer beckon me to sit, relax, and enjoy. That is what hospitality should be: warm, relaxing, and enjoyable to others. This antique cup and saucer were a gift—another reminder that hospitality is a gift we give those who enter our homes.

Above all, keep your love for one another at full strength, since "love covers a multitude of sins." Be hospitable to one another without complaining. Based on the gift they have received, everyone should use it to serve others. 1 Peter 4:8–10 (HCSB)

"Be careful not to practice your righteousness in front of people, to be seen by them. Otherwise, you will have no reward from your Father in heaven." Matthew 6:1 (HCSB)

See also Proverbs 15:17 (NASB); Galatians 5:13–14 (HCSB)

~

PRAYER

Dear loving Father, how I do love You. I thank You for loving me. Please help me to keep my love for others fervent and strong. I pray that I will be hospitable without complaining. I desire not to entertain for self-indulgent motives—such as to be noticed for my cooking or my decorating. Thank You for the gifts You have given me. Help me to use these gifts in loving service of others. In Jesus' name, *amen*.

Cultivating Friendships

(*Patti*) I still have my earthenware mug. Many years ago my friend purchased one for each of us from our favorite potter. We were to drink our hot beverages from them for the first time on my birthday. I had moved thousands of miles away. This was the first birthday we could not celebrate together since our friendship began. That early morning sip brought joy and sorrow—joy for the good memories, sorrow for miles that separated us now. Each time I hold this stoneware piece, warm memories rush over me. Friendships like these are rare.

A friend loves at all times. Proverbs 17:17a (NIV)

A man of many companions may come to ruin, but there is a friend who sticks closer than a brother. Proverbs 18:24 (NIV)

Wounds from a friend can be trusted. Proverbs 27:6 (NIV)

Iron sharpens iron, so one man sharpens another. Proverbs 27:17

Oil and perfume make the heart glad,
So a man's counsel is sweet to his friend. Proverbs 27:9

~

PRAYER

Oh God, I desire to be a good friend—a friend who loves at all times. Help me always to be available to my friends when they need me. Thank You that they encourage me with their sweet and pleasing words of wisdom. Thank You also that when their words sharpen and correct me, I can trust them. Help me to be a friend like that. May I be a sweet perfume that makes the heart glad. In the sweet name of Jesus, *amen.*

Accepting People Who Are Different

(*Patti*) My gift was lovely but unusual. I thought I would enjoy this teacup and saucer, but the cup was a little different from the others in my collection. This cup was off-white, not as refined as the other cups, and it had an unusual raised violet pattern encircling the rim.

A friend told me she had seen this style of china discussed on a home and garden show. The process of making the antique cup and saucer was long and tedious. The raised uneven patterns were made with many layers of firing. Thus the result was an unusual beauty.

I thought of people God has brought into my life who are different. At first glance I might not have appreciated their beauty within. But as God revealed layers of their lives, He showed me the refinement that life's firings had given them. People are sometimes like this special cup and saucer. At first glance they may seem unrefined and not worth our time. Time will reveal the depth of their beauty.

Don't be selfish; don't live to make a good impression on others. Be humble, thinking of others as better than yourself. Don't think only about your own affairs, but be interested in others, too, and what they are doing. Your attitude should be the same that Christ Jesus had.

Philippians 2:3–5 (NLT)

Your attitude should be the same that Christ Jesus had.

Do not be conformed to this age, but be transformed by the renewing of your mind, so that you may discern what is the good, pleasing, and perfect will of God. Romans 12:2 (HCSB)

Be in agreement with one another. Do not be proud; instead, associate with the humble. Do not be wise in your own estimation.
Romans 12:16 (HCSB)

"Give, and it will be given to you. A good measure, pressed down, shaken together and running over, will be poured into your lap. For with the measure you use, it will be measured to you."
Luke 6:38 (NIV)

See also Luke 6:36

~

PRAYER

Oh God, You said that I am always to think of others as better than myself. I am to think not only about my interests but also to be interested in others. I pray that You will convict me if I ever think I am wise in my own estimation. I desire not to be haughty or proud. My measure in this area is Christ Jesus Himself.

I pray that as I meet those who are different from me, I will not look at them from a worldly perspective—listening only to the opinions of others. Please transform my mind so I will view them from Your perspective. May I always treat everyone in ways that are good, pleasing, and acceptable to You. I realize that the way I treat others is not only a reflection on You but is also an example to others of the way I desire to be treated. In Jesus' name, *amen.*

Dear friends, if God loved us in this way, we also must love one another.

Giving My Love

The one who does not love does not know God, because God is love. . . .
Love consists in this: not that we loved God, but that He loved us
and sent His Son to be the propitiation for our sins. Dear friends,
if God loved us in this way, we also must love one another.
1 John 4:8, 10–11 (HCSB)

For the person who does not love his brother whom he has seen
cannot love God whom he has not seen. And we have this command
from Him: the one who loves God must also love his brother.
1 John 4:20b–21 (HCSB)

~

PRAYER

Dear loving Father, I can never get over the truth that You loved
me first. I love You; thank You for loving me. Whenever I do not
have love for someone who is different, please remind me that if I do
not love him or her, I do not love You. I desire to obey Your command to love my brother. In Jesus' name, *amen.*

Encouraging Others

Therefore encourage one another and build up one another,
just as you also are doing. 1 Thessalonians 5:11

But encourage one another day after day. Hebrews 3:13a

Let us hold unswervingly to the hope we profess, for he who promised
is faithful. And let us consider how we may spur one another on
toward love and good deeds. . . . Let us encourage one another.
Hebrews 10:23–25 (NIV)

He [Josiah] set the priests in their offices and encouraged them
in the service of the house of the LORD. 2 Chronicles 35:2

And Jonathan . . . went to David at Horesh, and encouraged him in God.
1 Samuel 23:16

May the God of hope fill you with all joy and peace as you trust in him,
so that you may overflow with hope by the power of the Holy Spirit.
Romans 15:13 (NIV)

~

PRAYER

Oh Father, may I be an encourager today. Help me to hold unswervingly to the hope I profess—my belief in Jesus Christ as my Savior and Lord. Help me to think of ways to spur others toward love and good deeds. May I encourage those who are serving You in their churches. May I encourage all my Christian friends to put their hope in You. Please fill me with Your joy and peace as I trust in You, so that my life will overflow with hope by the power of Your Spirit. In Jesus' name, *amen.*

A Lasting Gift

(*Sarah*) In the year 2000, Nashville, Tennessee, had the privilege of hosting a Billy Graham Crusade. In carrying out my responsibilities for the crusade, I worked closely with several women on the Billy Graham staff, all of whom were single. One day I decided to buy roses for them—just to say thank you for their diligent labors of love.

When I arrived at the florist, I discovered that by buying one bunch of twenty-five roses of any color, I would receive twenty-five red roses free. I was delighted. Now I could give the liaison twenty-five beautiful pink roses and each assistant a dozen red roses, with one to spare.

It was such a little thing for me to do; it required very little money or effort. But oh, was it worth it! One of the assistants told me she had never before received roses. The liaison was absolutely delighted with her pink roses. When I informed her that the vase was hers also, I learned that she had been looking for one just like it. As each rose faded, she added it to her basket of dried flowers. This gave me the assurance that the fragrance would linger on and on.

The gift of encouragement is like those roses. It meets special needs in surprising ways, and the fragrance lives on long after the gift is given. As women, we have so many opportunities to give the gift of encouragement. It may be through affirming words, acts of service, meaningful touches, or special gifts. When the Holy Spirit impresses our hearts that someone needs encouragement, we need to respond to His leading. In doing so, you and I will be able to splash joy on the people God has placed in our lives.

Practical Tip

PLANNING AN EVENT

1. Carefully plan for your event. (Make a detailed list of everything you need to do. Do as much ahead of time as possible.)

2. Collect materials to use again and again. (Organize napkins, napkin rings, placemats, tablecloths, centerpiece materials, etc. for easy accessibility.)

3. Clean your house on schedule. (Clean each room thoroughly before moving to the next.)

4. Cooperate with others in giving parties. (This makes it more fun.)

5. Clean up as you go. (When you make a mess, clean it up then, not later.)

6. Create as lovely a setting as possible. (A lovely setting does not have to be expensive.)

7. Commit every detail of your gathering to the Lord. (He desires to be a part of every event.)

8. Concentrate on the people who are in your home. (Everything doesn't have to be perfect.)

Even if you have not opened your home before, soon you'll be ready to say: "Y'all come in!" (Or "You guys come in!" if you are not a Southerner.)

Garden Tip

Always cut fresh rose stems under very warm water. This prevents air bubbles from forming. Add a pinch of sugar and a few drops of bleach to the water in the vase, and the blooms will last longer.

CHAPTER FIVE

Deepening My Roots
Growing Spiritually

*Only Jesus can transform us by His grace into a people
who are a reflection of His character.*

—Marijean Green, *Promises, Promises*

~

*G*od desires that we grow spiritually. We do this by letting our roots draw nourishment from the Lord Jesus Christ. Using God's Word, not the world's wisdom, as our plumbline, we discover that our competence and our righteousness are from Him. If we are to bear fruit, we must abide in Him and in His Word. Pruning will be necessary for optimum growth, but it will be worth it if we become more like Jesus.

*"My sheep hear My voice, I know them, and they follow Me.
I give them eternal life, and they will never perish—ever!
No one will snatch them out of My hand." John 10:27–28 (HCSB)*

*And now, just as you accepted Christ Jesus as your Lord, you must
continue to live in obedience to him. Let your roots grow down into
him and draw up nourishment from him, so you will grow in faith,
strong and vigorous in the truth you were taught. Let your lives
overflow with thanksgiving for all he has done. Colossians 2:6–9 (NLT)*

~

DAILY PRAYER

Lord Jesus, thank You for dying on the cross for my sins. By faith, I accepted You as my Savior and Lord. I praise You that I belong to You, and no one can ever snatch me out of Your hand.

It is my earnest desire to live a life of faith and obedience, overflowing with thanksgiving for all You have done. May I let my "roots" grow down into You and draw up nourishment from You. In this way my faith will grow strong and vigorous in the truth I have been taught. In Jesus' name, *amen.*

*Let your roots grow down
into Him and draw up
nourishment from Him . . .*

A Perspective of Praise

(*Patti*) I'll never forget January 15, 1990, the day I learned I had colon cancer. Those three little words, "You have cancer," were devastating. For years I had been happily occupied with raising my boys, meeting my husband's needs, teaching school, and being involved in exciting church opportunities. I found myself hating this "enemy within me." I did not want my comfortable life interrupted. In my innocence I had no idea the ways in which our lives would never be the same.

The next evening as I faced surgery, my hospital room was filled with family and friends. We laughed and prayed together. After they left, in the quiet of that empty room, fear swept over me like a flood. Questions paraded through my mind. What did the future hold? Would I live or die? My eyes rested on a book a friend had brought to me. God used this book on praise to highlight the Scripture: "This is what the LORD says to you: 'Do not be afraid or discouraged because of this vast army. For the battle is not yours, but God's.' . . . Jehoshaphat appointed men to sing to the LORD and to praise him for the splendor of his holiness . . . saying: 'Give thanks to the LORD, for his love endures forever.' As they began to sing and praise, the LORD set ambushes against [their enemies], and they were defeated" (2 Chron. 20:15b, 21–22, NIV). God used these verses to teach me about Himself that night. As I paced the hospital halls singing, praising, and focusing on God, my enemies—fear, anger, and bitterness—all melted away. I knew that as I trusted God's promise in Scripture, He would set His ambushes against my enemies. At that moment I was not fearful of the cancer or the future.

A month after surgery, I began the year-long chemotherapy regime. Soon I found my body "on fire" from the treatments. Tufts of hairs fell out daily. The medicine that was killing the cancer made my insides feel like I was racing; my physical energy was zero. For three months my daily routine began with getting out of bed and heading to the couch. There I would lie the entire day. I wasn't accomplishing a thing. Soon feelings of being worthless, useless, and nonproductive flowed through my being. Once more I determined not to be conquered by my feelings. As I focused on God and praised Him for who He was, He removed my fears.

As I was relegated to my couch, I saw my yard from a different perspective. My January surgery was my "winter." I dreamed about the many flowers I wanted to see from my windows. A friend gave me a bird feeder that drew beautiful birds to my yard. A dear Christian psychologist friend made a weekly phone appointment to help me focus on getting well. Another friend gave me quiet neighborhood tea parties on my patio. These times of retreat and rest helped me refocus my thoughts from the battle within to a focus on God and His beauty outside. As the flowers and trees budded, I saw "spring" coming to my spirit.

That was a year I shall never forget. My cancer was not the only crisis. My forty-year-old brother and his wife were killed in a head-on crash, leaving two small daughters. My father had a stroke and later died in a nursing home. With each crisis came a choice—either to praise God or to focus on the crisis. I chose to praise God. He used those praises to teach me about Himself. When I praise Him, I experience God changing my heart until I have a godly perspective on the situations before me.

Deepening My Roots
Means Dependence on God

When I Need Refuge

Call upon Me in the day of trouble; I shall rescue you,
and you will honor Me. Psalm 50:15

Be gracious to me, O God, . . . For my soul takes refuge in You;
And in the shadow of Your wings I will take refuge
Until destruction passes by. I will cry to God Most High,
. . . who accomplishes all things for me. Psalm 57:1–2

Rejoice in the Lord always. I will say it again: Rejoice! Let your
graciousness be known to everyone. The Lord is near. Don't worry about
anything, but in everything, through prayer and petition with
thanksgiving, let your requests be made known to God. And the peace
of God, which surpasses every thought, will guard your hearts and
your minds in Christ Jesus. Philippians 4:4–7 (HCSB)

The LORD is with me; he is my helper. I will look in triumph on my
enemies. It is better to take refuge in the Lord than to trust in man.
Psalm 118:7–8 (NIV)

The LORD is my strength, and my song; he has become my salvation.
Psalm 118:14 (NIV)

See also Psalm 62:8; Psalm 17:6; Psalm 118:28a–29b (NKJV)

PRAYER

Oh God, what a blessing to know that when I call on You in times of trouble, You are honored. Thank You that I can pour out my heart to You, and You will be my refuge. How I need to take refuge in You. I desire to rest in the shadow of Your wings until this difficult time has passed. You are the One who will accomplish all things for me. I thank You for this promise.

Father, I know Your Word says not to worry. But I am worried about this situation I am facing. I desire to be obedient. So with thanksgiving in my heart, I am asking You for _____. I praise You that as I give my requests to You, You will give me Your peace to guard my heart and mind.

You are my helper, Oh Lord. I will not trust in man. I will trust in You. You are my salvation, my strength, and my song. I praise You. In Jesus' name, *amen.*

When I Am Afraid

See, I have engraved you on the palms of my hands. Isaiah 49:16 (NIV)

When I am afraid, I will put my trust in You.
In God, whose word I praise, in God I have put my trust;
I shall not be afraid. What can mere man do to me? Psalm 56:3–4

But now, thus says the LORD, your Creator, O Jacob,
And He who formed you, O Israel, "Do not fear, for I have redeemed you;
I have called you by name; you are Mine! When you pass through the waters,

I will be with you; And through the rivers, they will not overflow you.
When you walk through the fire, you will not be scorched, nor will
the flame burn you." Isaiah 43:1–2

"So do not fear, for I am with you; do not be dismayed, for I am your God.
I will strengthen you and help you; I will uphold you
with my righteous right hand." Isaiah 41:10 (NIV)

PRAYER

Father, thank You that I am engraved on the palms of Your hands. Right now I am afraid. I desire to put my trust in You. As I walk through this difficult time, I will choose to praise You. At this moment I put my trust in You. You have called me by name, and I am Yours. That thought overwhelms me. What a comfort it is to know that when I pass through these troubling waters, You will be with me. They will not flow over me. I praise Your name that as I walk through this fire I will not be destroyed. Thank You for strengthening me and upholding me with Your righteous hand. In Jesus' holy name, *amen.*

In God, whose word I praise,
In God I have put my trust . . .

When I Need Stability

I have set the LORD always before me. Because he is at my right hand.
I will not be shaken. Therefore my heart is glad and my tongue rejoices;
my body also will rest secure. Psalm 16:8–9 (NIV)

Be strong and let your heart take courage,
All you who hope in the LORD. Psalm 31:24

By the Word of the LORD the heavens were made. Psalm 33:6a

~

PRAYER

Oh Father, I need Your stability. I need Your strength. I declare that
by Your Word the heavens were made. You made all things, and You
are in control. Because You are at my right hand, I will not be shaken.
I rejoice in You. I will rest in You and be secure. You are my hope. In
the mighty name of Jesus, *amen.*

When I Receive Bad News

They do not fear bad news; they confidently trust the LORD
to care for them. Psalm 112:7 (NLT)

God is our refuge and strength, a very present help in trouble.
Therefore we will not fear, though the earth should change
And though the mountains slip into the heart of the sea; . . .
The LORD of hosts is with us; the God of Jacob is our stronghold.
Psalm 46:1–2, 7

Dear God, this bad news is getting me down. I desire to trust You confidently to care for me. I do not want to focus on this event. I want instead to focus on the truth that You are my refuge and strength. You are always there to help me. I choose not to fear even though, like mountains slipping into the sea, my world is falling apart. You are my stronghold. I love You. In Jesus' name, *amen.*

Every branch in Me that does not produce fruit, He removes . . .

Deepening My Roots
Demands Constant Pruning

"I am the true vine, and My Father is the vineyard keeper.
Every branch in Me that does not produce fruit He removes, and He
prunes every branch that produces fruit so that it will produce more fruit."
John 15:1–2 (HCSB)

Consider it a great joy, my brothers, whenever you experience various
trials, knowing that the testing of your faith produces endurance.
But endurance must do its complete work, so that you may be mature
and complete, lacking nothing. James 1:2–4 (HCSB)

Oh God, I desire to "consider it all joy" when I experience trials. It is so difficult for me to rejoice in (*name the trial*). I acknowledge that You use such hard times to prune me so that I can be more fruitful. God, pruning hurts. Thank You that these difficult experiences will produce endurance. Then I will be mature and complete in You, lacking in nothing. In Jesus' name, *amen*.

Deepening My Roots Results in Growth

My Competence Is from Christ

We have this kind of confidence toward God through Christ: not that we are competent in ourselves to consider anything as coming from ourselves, but our competence is from God. 2 Corinthians 3:4–5 (HCSB)

His divine power has given us everything required for life and godliness, through the knowledge of Him who called us by His own glory and goodness. By these He has given us very great and precious promises, so that through them you may share in the divine nature, escaping the corruption that is in the world because of evil desires.

2 Peter 1:3–4 (HCSB)

PRAYER

Father, I know I am not competent to grow and learn on my own. I agree with You that my competency, my adequacy, is from You alone. Thank You that Your divine power has given me everything I require for life and godliness. I pray that You will guide me as I gain knowledge about You. Help me to be aware that with Your power I can choose not to participate in evil desires. In Jesus' name, *amen.*

My Righteousness Is from Christ Jesus Alone

I count all things to be loss in view of the surpassing value of knowing Christ Jesus my Lord, for whom I have suffered the loss of all things, and count them but rubbish so that I may gain Christ, and may be found in Him, not having a righteousness of my own derived from the Law, but that which is through faith in Christ, the righteousness which comes from God on the basis of faith, that I may know Him and the power of His resurrection and the fellowship of His sufferings, being conformed to His death. Philippians 3:8–10

~

PRAYER

Lord Jesus, as I look at my life, I see that my degrees, my talents, my training, and my background are nothing compared to what You are to me. You are Christ Jesus, my Lord. I can never be righteous on my own. My righteousness comes from You alone. I desire to know You, oh Christ, and the power of Your resurrection. In Your name, *amen.*

*... be transformed by
the renewing of your mind.*

My Transformation Reflects the Lord

*We all ... are reflecting the glory of the Lord and are being
transformed into the same image from glory to glory;
this is from the Lord who is the Spirit. 2 Corinthians 3:18 (HCSB)*

*"If you remain in me and my words remain in you, ask whatever you
wish, and it will be given you." John 15:7 (NIV)*

*Offer your bodies as living sacrifices, holy and pleasing to God ....
Do not conform any longer to the pattern of this world, but be transformed
by the renewing of your mind. Then you will be able to test and
approve what God's will is—his good, pleasing and perfect will.
Romans 12:1–2 (NIV)*

~

PRAYER

Dear God, thank You that through the power of the Holy Spirit, I
am being transformed daily to become more like You. I acknowledge
that this change comes about only as I let my mind be renewed—as I
let Your Word transform my thinking. Then I will know Your will and
can ask You anything because You will show me Your desires for my
life. In Jesus' holy name, *amen.*

My Fruit Comes from Abiding in Christ

"Abide in Me, and I in you. As the branch cannot bear fruit of itself, unless it abides in the vine, neither can you, unless you abide in Me. I am the vine, you are the branches. He who abides in Me, and I in him, bears much fruit; for without Me you can do nothing."
John 15:4–5 (NKJV)

[Jesus said] "I am in My Father, and you in Me, and I in you."
John 14:20b (NKJV)

~

PRAYER

Dear Lord Jesus, I rejoice that You live in me and I live in You. You are the source of my strength. I can do nothing without You. You are the vine. I am a branch. I desire to be fruitful. Jesus, my Savior, I acknowledge that I cannot bear fruit unless I abide in You. I want to learn from You and grow to know You more intimately. Help me. I want to glorify the Father and bear much fruit. In Jesus' name, *amen.*

He who abides in Me, and I in him, bears much fruit.

Deepening My Roots
Requires Forgiveness

Forgiving Others

All bitterness, anger and wrath, insult and slander must be removed from you, along with all wickedness. And be kind and compassionate to one another, forgiving one another, just as God also forgave you in Christ. Ephesians 4:31–32 (HCSB)

"And forgive us our debts, as we also have forgiven our debtors. . . . For if you forgive people their wrongdoing, your heavenly Father will forgive you as well. But if you don't forgive people, your Father will not forgive your wrongdoing." Matthew 6:12, 14–15 (HCSB)

If anyone has caused grief, he has not so much grieved me as he has grieved all of you, to some extent . . . Now instead, you ought to forgive and comfort him, so that he will not be overwhelmed by excessive sorrow. I urge you, therefore, to reaffirm your love for him . . . in order that Satan might not outwit us. For we are not unaware of his schemes. 2 Corinthians 2:5, 7–8, 11 (NIV)

See also Colossians 3:12–13

PRAYER

Dear God, these words of Yours are hard to obey. I am bitter and angry about the way _____ has treated (others or me). I know that I have a choice: to retain these feelings of bitterness or to remove them from my heart. You have spoken clearly that I am to forgive this person, just as You have forgiven me. You have also said that if I do not forgive others, my heavenly Father will not forgive me. I long to be obedient, but this is such a difficult command. Please help me, oh Lord. By an act of my will, I now choose to forgive _____.

Now, Father, show me how to obey an even more difficult command. Please enable me not only to extend forgiveness to _____ but also to be kind and compassionate toward (him or her). May I reaffirm my love to _____ so that Satan cannot take advantage of me in this situation. It is only in Your strength that I can do this. Thank You for empowering me. In Jesus' name, *amen.*

Forgiving Myself

Then I acknowledged my sin to you, and I did not hide my iniquity;
I said, "I will confess my transgressions to the LORD,"
and you forgave the guilt of my sin. Psalm 32:5 (NRSV)

Let the wicked forsake his way And the unrighteous man his thoughts;
And let him return to the LORD, and He will have compassion on
him, and to our God, for He will abundantly pardon. Isaiah 55:7

If we confess our sins, He is faithful and righteous to forgive us our sins
and to cleanse us from all unrighteousness. 1 John 1:9

PRAYER

Dear Father, thank You that when I confess my sins to You, You forgive the guilt of my sin and abundantly pardon me. Thank You for cleansing me from all unrighteousness. I acknowledge that sometimes it is hard to forgive myself. I pray that You will help me to take seriously the fact that You have forgiven me. Therefore, if You who are holy can forgive me, then I can rest in Your forgiveness and forgive myself. In Jesus' name, *amen*.

Practical Tip

(*Patti*) Writing and praying Scripture in my quiet times has changed my prayer life. It keeps me focused on God and His desires. He uses the Scriptures I record to teach me His thoughts. He then starts molding and changing me. These thoughts guide me as I intercede for others. I pray that this plan will encourage you to start your own journal. Use my suggestions as a beginning point. Develop your own method.

DEVELOPING A PRAYER JOURNAL

I use a 120-sheet spiral notebook as a prayer journal. I divide it into two sections set apart with tabs. The first section (80 sheets) is used for my personal journal entries to God. The second (40 sheets) is for my prayer list. I enter thoughts into my personal journal almost every day.

Section 1:
Personal Journal Entries

1. Write the date (include the year) at the beginning of your entry.

2. Write your thoughts to God. Praise Him. Tell Him your frustrations and joys. Confess your sins. (Don't worry about the order or your spelling and grammar.) If you do not feel like talking to God, tell Him. Always praise Him whether you feel like it or not.

3. Read a few verses of Scripture and record what you have read (indicate book, chapter, and verse). The Scriptures you record each day may be from a study you are doing, a systematic reading of a book of the Bible, or a topical study. Reflect on what you have recorded. In your own words, write these verses as a prayer back to God.

4. Record any insights you have gained from this Scripture. As God's Word permeates your thoughts, He often reveals sins that you need to confess. Write down what He is saying to you about that sin, ask for forgiveness and His power to change. If new praise erupts, record that.

This time with God prepares you to enter into a time of intercession using the prayer list section.

Section 2: Prayer List

Allot several pages for each category of your prayer list, marking each with a separate tab. Include your husband, children and their spouses, grandchildren, extended family, friends and others, missionaries, your church, your children's churches, yourself, and so forth. Your categories will reflect your life.

Write the Scriptures to pray for that person, followed by a list of specific requests. Record the date of each request and answer.

Come, all you who are thirsty, come to the waters; ...
Listen, listen to me, and eat what is good,
and your soul will delight in the richest of fare ...
Seek the LORD while he may be found;
call on him while he is near. Isaiah 55:1a, 2b, 6 (NIV)

Garden Tip

In the spring cut away old leaves and stems so air can move easily around the plant. This pruning will retard mildew growth. Your plants will produce strong, healthy new growth.

CHAPTER SIX

Working in My Garden

Honoring God in My Endeavors

*Wouldn't it make an astounding difference, not only in the quality
of the work we do (in office, schoolroom, factory, kitchen, or backyard), but also in our satisfaction, even our joy, if we recognized
God's gracious gift in every single task, from making a bed or
bathing a baby to drawing a blueprint or selling a computer?*

— Elisabeth Elliot, *Keep a Quiet Heart*

~

*E*very endeavor presents challenges to us as women, whether we
minister as a volunteer, through a career, and/or to our families. Each
task must be committed to the Lord for His leadership and guidance.
Through our actions, attitudes, and responses, we are to be examples
of God's grace in our relationships and in the daily situations we face.

Whatever you do, work at it with all your heart, as working for
the Lord, not for men, . . . It is the Lord Christ you are serving.
Colossians 3:23–24 (NIV)

~

DAILY PRAYER

Father, I pray for Your strength and guidance as I seek to do Your will in this endeavor. I desire to glorify You in all that I do. It is the Lord Christ I am serving. Sometimes it is easy to want to please others more than You. Help me to do this work with all my heart, giving it my best at all times. In Jesus' name, *amen.*

Advice from the Experts

(*Patti*) We were living in paradise. When you live in Hawaii, it is basically easy to grow beautiful vegetation in your yard. Mine was not the exception. I had poinsettias, plumaria trees, a mango tree, papaya trees, ti plants, an octopus tree, and banana plants. The previous occupants of our home had planted them. These plants flourished with little care from me.

My desire was to have indoor plants for the house also. Yet everything I grew started to die. Two special friends, Josefina Saludez and Stanley Kapepa, rescued me. They would take my plants, nurse them back to health, and return them to me. My friends knew plants and how to take care of them. They taught me what I was doing wrong with each one. As the years went by, fewer and fewer plants required their special attention.

When I moved to Nashville, Tennessee, I realized I faced a different problem. I had not lived in this part of the United States as an adult. I knew nothing about the plants or growing seasons. Once again I had to reach out to others for help. My friend and neighbor, Linda Dotson, had a lovely herb and flower garden. I sought her advice. Soon my yard was full of beautiful herbs and flowers.

I learned about plants in Hawaii and Nashville by seeking advice from experts. I had to swallow my pride and ask for advice. It is a principle to apply to any new challenge, such as a new career, projects, a new marriage, or parenthood. We must not let our pride keep us from seeking another person's help. We need to seek the counsel of those who have walked the path we are now walking. Whether it is advice from a person who has a career, a stay-at-home mom, or an active volunteer, they can help us see what is hindering our growth. We need to ask them to look at our lives and see if they have suggestions about how we can reflect God's glory in our new challenge. Asking for help or advice takes swallowing pride. But my garden of life will be enriched when I seek godly wisdom.

My flower garden today is not like Josefina's, Stanley's, or Linda's. Even though I sought their advice, I have developed my own special style and choice of flowers. I must always allow the Lord to show me the unique plans He has for me. I must let Him develop me as His creation.

Seeking God's Guidance
Concerning Our Endeavors

His Plans

The mind of man plans his way, But the LORD directs his steps. Proverbs 16:9

Commit your works to the LORD, and your plans will be established.
Proverbs 16:3

Always wrestling in prayer for you, that you may stand firm in all the
will of God, mature and fully assured. Colossians 4:12b (NIV)

"For I know the plans that I have for you," declares the LORD, "plans for
welfare and not for calamity to give you a future and a hope."
Jeremiah 29:11

See also Proverbs 2:6

~

PRAYER

Thank You, Lord, that You know the plans You have for me. I want
You to direct my steps. I commit this endeavor to You so that Your
plans will be established. I desire to stand firm in Your will and to be
mature and fully assured in the new challenge before me. Please give
me Your wisdom. In Your name I pray, *amen.*

His Priorities

"But seek first the kingdom of God and His righteousness,
and all these things will be provided for you." Matthew 6:33 (HCSB)

Therefore be careful how you walk, not as unwise men, but as wise, making the most of your time, because the days are evil. So then do not be foolish, but understand what the will of the Lord is. Ephesians 5:15–17

Direct my footsteps according to your word; let no sin rule over me. Psalm 119:133 (NIV)

~

PRAYER

Dear Father, it is my desire for You to be at the controls of my life today. I want You to direct my steps according to Your Word. I know that if I try to go my own way, I am being foolish. Help me to hear Your voice above all others. Help me to walk as a wise woman, not an unwise one, making the most of my time. Please help me to seek first Your kingdom and Your priorities for my life. In Jesus' name, *amen.*

For it is God who is at work in you . . .

Allowing God to Work in and Through Me

Being Equipped

For it is God who is at work in you, both to will and to work for His good pleasure. Philippians 2:13

May the God of peace, who through the blood of the eternal covenant brought back from the dead our Lord Jesus . . . equip you with everything good for doing his will, and may he work in us what is pleasing to him, through Jesus Christ, to whom be glory for ever and ever. Hebrews 13:20–21 (NIV)

PRAYER

Oh Father, as I begin this _____ (new endeavor), I ask that I will be aware of Your working in me to bring glory to You. I am excited that You can equip me with everything I need to do Your will in this matter, if I allow You to do so. It is my sincere desire to please You in every endeavor. In Jesus' name, *amen.*

Giving My Best to My Work

Whatsoever thy hand findeth to do, do it with thy might.
Ecclesiastics 9:10 (KJV)

Whatever you do in word or deed, do all in the name of the Lord Jesus,
giving thanks through Him to God the Father . . . Whatever you do,
do your work heartily, as for the Lord rather than for men.
Colossians 3:17, 23

~

PRAYER

Father, as I begin this day, help me to do my work heartily, being aware that I am doing it for You rather than for man. Whatever I am called on to do, may I do it with all my might. May I remember that all I do and say is to be done in the name of the Lord Jesus, with a spirit of gratitude in my heart. In Jesus' name, *amen.*

Being a Woman of Godly Character

INTEGRITY

He who walks in integrity walks securely,
But he who perverts his ways will be found out. Proverbs 10:9

My lips certainly will not speak unjustly, nor will my tongue mutter
deceit . . . Till I die I will not put away my integrity from me. Job 27:4, 5b

See also Proverbs 11:3

HONESTY

Lying lips are an abomination to the LORD, but those who deal
truthfully are His delight. Proverbs 12:22 (NKJV)

Pray for us, for we are sure that we have a good conscience, desiring to
conduct ourselves honorably in all things. Hebrews 13:18

DISCIPLINE

Like a city that is broken into and without walls
Is a man who has no control over his spirit. Proverbs 25:28

Now for this very reason also, applying all diligence, in your faith
supply moral excellence, and in your moral excellence, knowledge,
and in your knowledge, self-control, and in your self-control,
perseverance, and in your perseverance, godliness. 2 Peter 1:5–6

DILIGENCE

Whatever you do, do your work heartily, as for the Lord
rather than for men. Colossians 3:23

Work hard and become a leader; be lazy and never succeed.
Proverbs 12:24 (TLB)

Teach me good discernment and knowledge,
For I believe in Your commandments. Psalm 119:66

I pray, that your love may abound still more and more in knowledge
and all discernment, that you may approve the things that are excel-
lent, that you may be sincere and without offense till the day of Christ.
Philippians 1:9–10 (NKJV)

~

PRAYER

Oh my Father, I long to be a woman of godly character. May I walk in integrity. Help me to deal honestly with every person I encounter. I truly desire to keep a good conscience. May moral excellence and self-control be consistent characteristics of my daily life. I want to be a hard worker, working heartily for You rather than for man. Help me to be discerning, seeking to use good judgment in every situation. Oh Father, please reveal to me any areas in which I am not walking as You would have me walk. I do want to be sincere and without offense until the day Christ returns. In Jesus' name, *amen.*

Relating Properly to My Coworkers

In My Responses

Everyone should be quick to listen, slow to speak
and slow to become angry. James 1:19 (NIV)

A gentle answer turns away wrath, but a harsh word stirs up anger.
Proverbs 15:1

He who gives an answer before he hears, it is folly and shame to him.
Proverbs 18:13

"Do to others as you would have them do to you." Luke 6:31 (NIV)

Do not repay anyone evil for evil. Be careful to do what is right in the eyes of everybody. If it is possible, as far as it depends on you, live at peace with everyone. Do not take revenge, . . . for it is written: "It is mine to avenge; I will repay," says the Lord. Romans 12:17–19 (NIV)

Be patient with everyone. Make sure that nobody pays back wrong for wrong, but always try to be kind to each other and to everyone else.
1 Thessalonians 5:14b–15 (NIV)

Let your speech always be gracious, seasoned with salt, so that you may know how you ought to answer everyone. Colossians 4:6 (NRSV)

See also Luke 6:27–28 (NIV)

PRAYER

Dear heavenly Father, please help me today in my responses. May I be quick to listen, slow to speak, and slow to become angry. May I not give an answer before I have really listened to what the other person has to say. May I be patient and kind, not using harsh words but gentle ones. May I respond to others as I would want them to respond to me, never repaying evil for evil. Oh Father, I cannot do this in my own strength. I will depend on You to empower me in this area today. Thank You, oh Lord. In Jesus' name I pray, *amen.*

In Times of Frustration

Therefore do not let your good be spoken of as evil.
Romans 14:16 (NKJV)

In all things show yourself to be . . . sound in speech which is beyond reproach, so that the opponent will be put to shame, having nothing bad to say about us. Titus 2:7–8

~

PRAYER

Dear God, I am frustrated about _____. I know that I can be above reproach only as I respond to this situation with Your power and guidance. I pray that no one will have a reason to speak evil of my words or actions. I pray that the person causing this difficulty will become aware of the problem she is causing. In Jesus' name, *amen.*

Being under Authority

Slaves, be obedient to those who are your masters according to the flesh, with fear and trembling, in the sincerity of your heart, as to Christ; not by way of eyeservice, as men-pleasers, but as slaves of Christ, doing the will of God from the heart. With good will render service, as to the Lord, and not to men. Ephesians 6:5–7

Obey your leaders and submit to their authority. They keep watch over you as men who must give an account. Obey them so that their work will be a joy, not a burden, for that would be of no advantage to you.
Hebrews 13:17 (NIV)

PRAYER

Dear Father, I am having difficulty with the person in authority over me. I do not respect her. I do not agree with the way she is handling her responsibilities.

When she is unfairly critical of my endeavors, Lord, help me keep my eyes on You. You have told me to be obedient to the one who is in authority over me. I realize that she must give an account to You and not to me. I pray that You will give me wisdom to submit to her authority so that her work will be a joy, not a burden. Please help me, oh God, with this challenge. In Jesus' holy name, *amen.*

Practical Tips

A GARDEN PLAN

Here's what you need for your new spring garden:[1]

Plant three rows of squash
1. Squash gossip
2. Squash criticism
3. Squash indifference

Plant seven rows of peas
1. Prayer
2. Promptness
3. Perseverance
4. Politeness
5. Preparedness
6. Purity
7. Patience

Plant seven heads of lettuce
1. Let us be unselfish and loyal.
2. Let us be faithful to duty.
3. Let us search the Scripture.
4. Let us not be weary in well doing.
5. Let us be obedient in all things.
6. Let us be truthful.
7. Let us love one another.

No garden is complete without turnips
1. Turn up with a smile, even when things are difficult.
2. Turn up with determination to do your best in God's service.

After planting, may you "grow in the grace and knowledge of our Lord and Savior Jesus Christ" (2 Pet. 3:18a) and may you reap rich results.

Garden Tip

Deadheading is important for most flowers. You must cut off the dead flowers so new flowers can easily grow and take their place. Carry a little basket or trash bag on your arm. As you cut the old flower, let it fall into the bag. This minimizes cleanup.

CHAPTER SEVEN

Applying God's Fertilizer

Enriching My Marriage

God gives wives one of the greatest secrets to being fulfilled as women: He encourages us to adorn ourselves with a "gentle and quiet spirit" which He says is very precious in His sight (1 Pet. 3:4). It is also precious in the sight of our husbands.

— Darlene Wilkinson, Promises, Promises

God desires that our marriages reflect His love, grace, and power. He wants to empower us to be the wives our husbands need. This will happen only as we allow Him to fill us with His Holy Spirit. Only then will we be able to manifest love, joy, peace, patience, kindness, goodness, faithfulness, gentleness, and self-control—the fruit of the Spirit.

And this is my prayer: that your love may abound more and more in knowledge and depth of insight, so that you may be able to discern what is best and may be pure and blameless until the day of Christ, filled with the fruit of righteousness that comes through Jesus Christ—to the glory and praise of God. Philippians 1:9–11 (NIV)

~

DAILY PRAYER

Oh heavenly Father, this is my prayer. I so want our lives as a couple to bring glory and praise to You. May our love for You and for one another abound more and more, so that we will keep on growing in our knowledge and depth of insight. Help us to look to You, so that we can discern what is best, and live pure, blameless lives. I know that only through Jesus Christ can we be filled with the fruit of righteousness. May we depend on Your enabling power every day of our lives. In Jesus' precious name, *amen.*

Nourishing Our Relationships

(*Patti*) My neighbor asked if I would help her plant some flowers in her yard. Together we dug up the hard clay soil. We realized at once that for healthy blossoms to grow, there must be additions to the dirt. There must be a proper balance of nitrogen, phosphate, potassium, and other trace elements to have a good growing medium. We knew that if the soil was deficient in any one of these elements, the plants would not be healthy. A one-time application of the fertilizer was not sufficient. For her garden to continue to flourish, the nutrients had to be frequently replaced.

Our marriages are a lot like gardens—they need constant care to flourish. They need to be cultivated and tenderly cared for. They need regular applications of "soul fertilizer" for maximum growth. What is this "soul fertilizer?" It is God's Word.

Just as regular applications of fertilizer are necessary for optimum plant health, so the application of God's "fertilizer for the soul" is a necessity for a healthy Christian marriage. As we regularly look into God's Word, obey His commands, and make applications of this "fertilizer" to our marriages, our marital relationships will flourish.

Being a Wife of Excellence

He who finds a wife finds what is good and receives favor from the LORD.
Proverbs 18:22 (NIV)

An excellent wife, who can find? For her worth is far above jewels.
The heart of her husband trusts in her, and he will have no lack of gain.
She does him good and not evil all the days of her life.
Proverbs 31:10–12

I will be careful to lead a blameless life . . . I will walk in my house with
blameless heart. I will set before my eyes no vile thing. Psalm 101:2–3 (NIV)

Better to live in a desert than with a quarrelsome and ill-tempered wife.
Proverbs 21:19 (NIV)

Your beauty should not come from outward adornment. . . . Instead, it
should be that of your inner self, the unfading beauty of a gentle and
quiet spirit, which is of great worth in God's sight. 1 Peter 3:3–4 (NIV)

Wives, submit to your husbands as to the Lord. For the husband is the head of the wife as Christ is the head of the church, his body, of which he is the Savior. Ephesians 5:22–23 (NIV)

"Haven't you read," he replied, "that at the beginning the Creator made them 'male and female,' and said, 'For this reason a man will leave his father and mother and be united to his wife, and the two will become one flesh'? So they are no longer two, but one. Therefore what God has joined together, let not man separate." Matthew 19:4–6 (NIV)

For it is God who is at work in you, both to will and to work for His good pleasure. Philippians 2:13

And God is able to make all grace abound to you, so that always having all sufficiency in everything, you may have an abundance for every good deed. 2 Corinthians 9:8

~

PRAYER

Dear Father, I want my husband to believe that in finding me, he has found something good. I long to be a wife of excellence. It is my earnest desire to do him good and not evil all the days of his life. I want to be a wife in whom my husband can always place his full confidence.

Help me, dear Lord, to be careful to walk in our house with a blameless heart, setting no vile thing before my eyes. Please help me also to have a gentle and quiet spirit. I do not want to be a quarrelsome, ill-tempered wife.

May I truly love _____ as my sweetheart and spiritual leader, being submissive to him as to the Lord. Oh Father, this is so difficult. It is only as I depend on Your strength that I can follow Your plan for our marriage. Please work in me both to will and to do Your good pleasure. I want so much to please You, Lord.

Help me daily to remember my vows to You and to _____. He is to be mine, and I am to be his for as long as we live. What you have joined together, I am not to separate. I ask You today to fill me with Your power for this awesome task. Oh Father, I look to You for the abundance of grace I need to fulfill my role as a godly wife. In Your precious name I pray, *amen.*

. . . The wife is to respect her husband.

Building Up My Husband

The wise woman builds her house, but with her own hands the foolish one tears hers down. Proverbs 14:1 (NIV)

Do not let any unwholesome talk come out of your mouths, but only what is helpful for building others up according to their needs, that it may benefit those who listen. . . . Get rid of all bitterness, rage and anger, brawling and slander, along with every form of malice. Be kind and compassionate to one another, forgiving each other, just as in Christ God forgave you. Ephesians 4:29, 31–32 (NIV)

To sum up, each one of you is to love his wife as himself, and the wife is to respect her husband. Ephesians 5:33 (HCSB)

For this reason a man will leave his father and mother and be joined to his wife, and the two will become one flesh. Ephesians 5:31 (HCSB)

Marriage must be respected by all, and the marriage bed kept undefiled, because God will judge immoral people and adulterers. Hebrews 13:4 (HCSB)

The husband should fulfill his marital duty to his wife, and likewise the wife to her husband. The wife's body does not belong to her alone but also to her husband. In the same way, the husband's body does not belong to him alone but also to his wife. 1 Corinthians 7:3–4 (NIV)

So that they may encourage the young women to love their husbands and children. Titus 2:4 (HCSB)

I am able to do all things through Him who strengthens me. Philippians 4:13 (HCSB)

~

PRAYER

Dear heavenly Father, I want so much to be a wise woman today—one who builds her house, not one who foolishly tears it down with her own hands. May no unwholesome words come forth from my lips today but only those which will build up _____, according to his needs. May I deal with any bitterness, anger, and wrath I may be harboring in my heart. After confessing and forsaking these negative emotions, may I replace them with positive actions of kindness and compassion. May I have a forgiving spirit in every situation, remembering Your loving forgiveness of me.

Oh Lord, I want to honor _____ as my spiritual leader. Help me, both publicly and privately, to acknowledge and respect his God-given position as the head of our home. May he learn how to love me like Christ loved the church.

You created the desire for intimacy in marriage. May I never forget that we are now one flesh. I belong to _____, and he belongs to me. May I honor my commitment to God and to him to keep my marriage vows. Please help me to communicate fully my love to him today, both in word and in deed.

May I never forget that I can only fulfill my God-given role as his wife through the strength of Christ, who lives within me. I am looking to You, dear Lord, for Your strength and empowerment today. In Jesus' name I pray, *amen.*

Your godly lives will speak to them better than any words.

Praying for My Husband

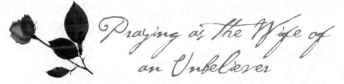

Praying as the Wife of an Unbeliever

In the same way, you wives must accept the authority of your husbands, even those who refuse to accept the Good News. Your godly lives will speak to them better than any words. They will be won over by watching your pure, godly behavior. 1 Peter 3:1–2 (NLT)

~

PRAYER

Dear Father, I so desire that my husband come to know You as his Lord and Savior. As I wait and pray, please help me to accept the authority of my husband. I desire that he be won over by my godly example. I praise You. You are indeed King of Kings and Lord of Lords (Rev. 19:16). In Your name, *amen.*

Therefore consider carefully how you listen.

Praying as the Wife of a Believer

"Therefore consider carefully how you listen." Luke 8:18a (NIV)

Such confidence as this is ours through Christ before God.
Not that we are competent in ourselves to claim anything for ourselves,
but our competence comes from God. 2 Corinthians 3:4–5 (NIV)

I keep asking that the God of our Lord Jesus Christ, the glorious Father,
may give you the Spirit of wisdom and revelation, so that you may know
him better. I pray also that the eyes of your heart may be enlightened in
order that you may know the hope to which he has called you, the riches
of his glorious inheritance in the saints, and his incomparably great
power for us who believe. Ephesians 1:17–19 (NIV)

PRAYER

Dear Lord, I thank You that my husband is a Christian. I pray that he will listen carefully to Your Word. I desire that he grow spiritually. May his confidence and competence always be in You and not in himself.

Oh God, give him the spirit of wisdom and revelation so that he will know You better. Please keep his eyes focused and clear so that he will comprehend the hope of Your calling on his life and the awesome power You give him. In Your blessed name, *amen.*

Praying for My Husband's Daily Life

I pray that He may grant you, according to the riches of His glory,
to be strengthened with power through His Spirit in the inner man.
Ephesians 3:16 (HCSB)

We are asking that you may be filled with the knowledge of His will
in all wisdom and spiritual understanding, so that you may walk
worthy of the Lord, fully pleasing to Him. Colossians 1:9b–10a (HCSB)

A good name is more desirable than great riches. Proverbs 22:1 (NIV)

May those who hope in you not be disgraced because of me, O Lord.
Psalm 69:6a (NIV)

And Jabez called on the God of Israel saying,
"Oh, that You would bless me indeed, and enlarge my territory,
that Your hand would be with me, and that You would keep me from evil,
that I may not cause pain!" 1 Chronicles 4:10 (NKJV)

~

PRAYER

Dear Father God, please strengthen my husband with power through Your Spirit in his inner being. Fill him with the knowledge of Your will in all wisdom and spiritual understanding so that he may be fully pleasing to You and walk worthy of You.

I pray that he will have a good name among the people with whom he works. May those who hope in You not be disgraced because of his actions. Bless him indeed, enlarge his territory, let Your hand be with him, and keep him from evil. In the wonderful name of Jesus, *amen.*

Practical Tip

1. For a month, read 1 Corinthians 13 every day. Use different translations. Ask God to reveal the aspect of loving that is the most difficult for you. Work on becoming the loving wife God desires you to be.

2. Write a love letter to your husband (or buy an appropriate card), expressing your love and appreciation for him.

3. Remember the three *As* a man needs from his wife:

Acceptance   *Affirmation*   *Adoration*

However, let each man of you [without exception] love his wife as [being in a sense] his very own self; and let the wife see that she respects and reverences her husband [that she notices him, regards him, honors him, prefers him, venerates, and esteems him; and that she defers to him, praises him, and loves and admires him exceedingly].
Ephesians 5:33 (Amplified)

Garden Tip

When planting geraniums, add ½ cup Epsom salts to the soil, mixing it in well. The salts will give your flowers a fast-growing boost. Later on, when feeding your geraniums, add 1 tablespoon of Epsom salts to each gallon of water. You will have beautiful blooms.

CHAPTER EIGHT

Growing Beautiful Plants

Experiencing Motherhood

Just as proper nutrition is needed for children to develop strong and healthy bodies, the pure milk of God's Word is vital to nourish the heart and character of every child. And God uses a parent's love not only to teach and instruct, but also to wrap a child's heart with the warmth of comfort, protection and blessing.

—Karla Dornacher, Love in Every Room

Being a mother is hard. As we raise our children, it is easy to be distracted by the world's ideas of what is important. God's Word is to be our child-raising manual. He has the blueprint for their lives. We must constantly be on our knees, praying for the wisdom and strength to fulfill this awesome responsibility God has given us.

May our sons flourish in their youth like well-nurtured plants.
May our daughters be like graceful pillars, carved to beautify a palace. . . .
Happy indeed are those whose God is the LORD. Psalm 144:12, 15b (NLT)

DAILY PRAYER

Oh Father, what an awesome responsibility it is to be a mother. It is my desire to see my sons flourish like well-nurtured plants. I long to see my daughters be like the graceful pillars that beautify a palace. But this will not happen if I do not follow Your plan in raising them. How I need Your wisdom to teach and train them in the way they should go.

I am looking to You, oh Abba Father, to instruct and guide me with Your eye upon me (Ps. 32:8). You, oh Lord, are my God! May I always remember that in You alone will we, as a family, find true happiness. In Jesus' name, *amen.*

Raising Children in Good Ground

But he that received seed into the good ground is he that heareth the word, and understandeth it; which also beareth fruit, and bringeth forth, some an hundredfold, some sixty, some thirty. Matthew 13:23 (KJV)

(*Melana Hunt Monroe*) Days of excruciating exhaustion, grueling lifting and shoveling, dirty, nasty hands, streaked, sweaty face. Afternoon glances at ugly fingernails, limp, damp, gritty hair clinging to face and neck, scratches and fire-ant bites. Thirst. Early mornings heaving cumbersome bags of manure, peat, and humus from the car to the backyard.

This is the price—to someone—of a peaceful garden, filled with the spectrum of colors and textures of flowers, paths with flow and form, and hidden fragrances that together create a whisper of paradise.

Creating good ground for children's roots parallels working the soil in a garden. Without good ground a fortune spent on the plants themselves is pointless; expensive plants in bad soil will not thrive, but a seedling in dark, moist earth can hardly be stunted.

Likewise children thrive as God intended when given good ground well fertilized with love, prayer, discipline, and stability. Crucial, hidden roots grow first, eventually yielding tender blossoms and mature fruit.

Gardening pictures the season of child training for mothers. In the early stages of garden tending and parenting, the labor is intensive and demanding, with little to show for the work. Sometimes it is just plain dirty and hard. Outside of getting a peek of a bulb beginning to push through the soil, the first tasks of gardening thrive on the imagination of what will come. A sweet baby-fat smile, an earnest bedtime prayer, or a delighted giggle of discovery give the same impetus for motherhood to persevere.

Motherhood and gardening produce rewards that culminate with harvest. At the end of the season—both in child rearing and in gardening—joy and peaceful fulfillment make the hard work worthwhile. Stable, productive adult children who love and serve Christ yield more joy to parents than they could have envisioned at the "dirt and ant" stage. And much more importantly, from heaven's view, this process gives joy and glory to the One who created both Eden and the sons and daughters of Eve.

Praying for Myself as a Mother

That I May Have Wisdom and Discernment

When you ask, you do not receive, because you ask with wrong motives, that you may spend what you get on your pleasures. James 4:3 (NIV)

If any of you is lacking in wisdom, ask God, who gives to all generously and ungrudgingly, and it will be given you. James 1:5 (NRSV)

That your love may abound more and more in knowledge and depth of insight, so that you may be able to discern what is best. Philippians 1:9–10a (NIV)

I will instruct you and teach you in the way you should go; I will counsel you and watch over you. Psalm 32:8 (NIV)

~

PRAYER

Father, I lack wisdom in how to pray about this situation. Help me discern what is best. I do not want to ask with wrong motives. Thank You, Father, that as I seek to deal wisely with my children and grandchildren, You will instruct me and teach me in the way I should go. In Jesus' name, *amen*.

That I May Teach about God

"You shall love the LORD your God with all your heart, with all your
soul, and with all your strength. And these words which I command
you today shall be in your heart. You shall teach them diligently to
your children, and shall talk of them when you sit in your house,
when you walk by the way, when you lie down, and when you rise up."
Deuteronomy 6:5–7 (NKJV)

Hear now, O Israel, the decrees and laws I am about to teach you . . .
Teach them to your children and to their children after them.
Deuteronomy 4:1a, 9b (NIV)

~

PRAYER

Father, You have told me that it is my responsibility as a parent to diligently teach my children Your laws and commands. I desire to do this.
Show me how to teach my children Your Word. In Jesus' name, *amen.*

That I May Be an Example... In My Walk

Blessed are they whose ways are blameless, who walk
according to the law of the LORD. Psalm 119:1 (NIV)

The righteous man leads a blameless life;
blessed are his children after him. Proverbs 20:7 (NIV)

Oh that they had such a heart in them, that they would fear Me, and
keep all My commandments always, that it may be well with them
and with their sons forever! Deuteronomy 5:29

PRAYER

Dear God, I desire to be a godly woman in my walk—one who leads a blameless life. I want to have a heart that fears You, so that my children will be blessed. I desire to keep Your commandments always so that it may be well with them. In Jesus' name, *amen.*

In My Home

Pay careful attention, then, to how you walk—not as unwise people [women] but as wise—making the most of the time, because the days are evil. Ephesians 5:15–16 (HCSB)

She watches over the affairs of her household and does not eat the bread of idleness. Her children arise and call her blessed; her husband also, and he praises her. Proverbs 31:27–28 (NIV)

Do not love the world or the things that belong to the world. 1 John 2:15a (HCSB)

He who fears the LORD has a secure fortress, and for his children it will be a refuge. Proverbs 14:26 (NIV)

But rather determine this—not to put an obstacle or a stumbling block in a brother's way. Romans 14:13b

Do everything without grumbling and arguing, so that you may be blameless and pure, children of God who are faultless in a crooked and perverted generation, among whom you shine like stars in the world.
Philippians 2:14–15 (HCSB)

Oh Father, I want to be a wise woman who makes the most of her time. I do not want to be lazy. I desire to be a disciplined and diligent homemaker—one who watches carefully over the affairs of her household. Nor do I want to love the things of this world. But that is so difficult in the day in which we live. Only with Your strength and power will I be able to refuse worldly enticements.

Lord, I so desire that my home be a refuge for my children. Help me to remember that they learn so much from my example. May I never be a stumbling block to them. I want them to be able to see me as a "shining star" in this dark world. I pray that some day they will rise up and call me blessed. In Jesus' name, *amen*.

In My Counsel

He [Ahaziah] also walked in the ways of the house of Ahab,
for his mother was his counselor to do wickedly. 2 Chronicles 22:3

PRAYER

Oh God, I pray that I will never knowingly or unknowingly counsel my son or daughter to do wickedly. In Jesus' name, *amen*.

Her children arise and call her blessed;
her husband also, and he praises her.

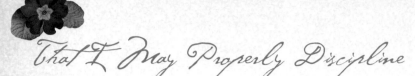

That I May Properly Discipline

Furthermore, we had natural fathers discipline us, and we respected them. Shouldn't we submit even more to the Father of spirits and live? For they disciplined us for a short time based on what seemed good to them, but He does it for our benefit, so that we can share His holiness. Hebrews 12:9–10 (HCSB)

*He who withholds his rod hates his son,
But he who loves him disciplines him diligently. Proverbs 13:24*

Fathers, don't stir up anger in your children, but bring them up in the training and instruction of the Lord. Ephesians 6:4 (HCSB)

~

PRAYER

Father, You have told me to train my child diligently through discipline. _____ has disobeyed me. I love him. I do not want to exasperate him. Give me wisdom to know what form of punishment to use so he will learn from his mistakes.

I want to follow Your example in disciplining my children. You always discipline me for my benefit; I desire to do the same for my child. In Jesus' name, *amen.*

To all generations I will make known Your faithfulness with my mouth.

Praying for Myself as a Grandmother

*The L*ORD *bless you out of Zion . . . All the days of your life.*
*Yes, may you see your children's children. Psalm 128:5–6a (*NKJV*)*

Grandchildren are the crown of old men,
And the glory of sons is their fathers. Proverbs 17:6

I will open my mouth in parables, I will utter hidden things,
things from of old—what we have heard and known, what our
fathers have told us. We will not hide them from their children;
*we will tell the next generation the praiseworthy deeds of the L*ORD*,*
*his power, and the wonders he has done. Psalm 78:2–4 (*NIV*)*

*I will sing of the lovingkindness of the L*ORD *forever; to all generations*
I will make known Your faithfulness with my mouth. Psalm 89:1

*See also Psalm 71:18 (*NKJV*)*

PRAYER

Thank You that my grandchildren are my crown. Give me wisdom,
Lord, to know how to tell this next generation about You. Show me
how to share Your praiseworthy deeds and the truths you have taught
me about Yourself. Oh God, give me strength to sing of Your loving-
kindness. I desire to tell my children's children of Your faithfulness.
In Jesus' name, *amen*.

Practical Tip

PRAYING FOR YOUR GRANDCHILDREN

1. Pray that you will be the grandmother God desires you to be. Pray for wisdom to develop a loving relationship with each grandchild.

2. As soon as you learn that a new grandchild is to be born, begin praying for him or her. Pray for his salvation. Pray that she, like Jesus, will increase in wisdom, in stature, and in favor with God and man. (See *A Mother's Garden of Prayer* for additional prayer ideas.[1])

3. At an appropriate age, share with your grandchildren the ways in which you are praying for them. Ask them for additional prayer suggestions.

4. When your grandchild is ten or eleven, begin to pray aloud with him concerning his future mate. Use Scriptures in your prayers.

5. In your prayer journal, have a section for each grandchild. Have her place her hand on one page and draw around it. Tell her that when you pray for her, you will place your hand on hers.

The above activities can be done even if your grandchildren live a long distance away. Use E-mail, postal services, or telephone. Be creative.

Garden Tip

In the fall after you purchase spring bulbs, store the bulbs in the refrigerator while you are waiting for the first hard freeze. If apples are also in the refrigerator, make sure that the bulbs are in a brown paper bag. Apples emit a gas that retards the growth of spring bulbs.

CHAPTER NINE

My Changing Garden

Growing Through Life's Seasons

When we don't know what, when, where, or how, we can trust in
Who. We won't always find our answers, but we can always find our
God when we seek Him with all our hearts. And He will love and
comfort us until all other answers come.

— Beth Moore, *To Live Is Christ*

~

One thing is certain: Change is inevitable; and for most of us,
change brings adjustments. Sometimes our lives are turned upside
down in an instant through an accident or death. Then there are
gradual changes such as growing older, children leaving home, and
the birth of grandchildren. God can enable us to celebrate His presence through all these changes, as we put our trust in Him.

"I the LORD, do not change." Malachi 3:6a (NIV)

*Every good thing given and every perfect gift is from above,
coming down from the Father of lights, with whom
there is no variation or shifting shadow. James 1:17*

*And God will generously provide all you need. Then you will always
have everything you need and plenty left over to share with others.
2 Corinthians 9:8 (NLT)*

*And God is able to make all grace abound to you, so that always
having all sufficiency in everything, you may have an abundance
for every good deed. 2 Corinthians 9:8*

~

DAILY PRAYER

Oh Father, everything around me seems to be changing—my body, my family, my world. How grateful I am that You, Lord, never change. Therefore, regardless of the changes that occur in my life, I know I can trust You to keep on taking care of me just as You have in the past. I thank You that You will generously provide all that I need. You will "make all grace abound to me." Then I will have plenty for myself as well as for others. In Jesus' name, *amen.*

And God will generously provide all you need.

The Joys of Change

(*Patti*) My Aunt Edna and Uncle Ray lived all their married lives in Knoxville, Tennessee. I have such fond memories of them and their four homes—especially their gardens.

At their first home on Lutrell Street, we had fun playing in the small side yard and flower garden. I still love seeing the photographs of my cousins and me (at three) hunting for Easter eggs in the emerging spring flowers.

Their next home on Cross Valley Road was larger, with an expansive lawn and pretty flower beds. My cousins and I have warm memories of playing games on that manicured lawn.

Then they moved to their third home on Scenic View Drive. My senses are flooded with the beauty of the placement of seasonal flowers and the huge vegetable garden. My children played in that yard while I watched.

But the sweetest garden is the one my aunt has now. She and Uncle Ray started growing flowers in the little plot of land just outside their first-floor condominium. Now widowed, my aunt tends that garden alone. The colorful flowers are a welcome sight to all who walk by.

Just as our gardens change, so do our lives. Once my aunt's home bulged with family members. Now she lives alone. As her circumstances have changed, adjustments have been necessary. When you and I undergo personal challenges, experience declining stamina, or move to different locations, we have to make adjustments. But with each change, through God's power, we can experience new joys.

The Onset of Aging

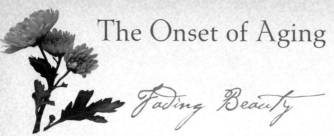

Fading Beauty

"Do not look at his appearance or at the height of his stature, because I have rejected him; for God sees not as man sees, for man looks at the outward appearance, but the LORD looks at the heart." 1 Samuel 16:7

Gray hair is a crown of glory; it is gained in a righteous life. Proverbs 16:31 (NRSV)

Charm is deceptive, and beauty is fleeting; but a woman who fears the LORD is to be praised. Proverbs 31:30 (NIV)

"You shall have no other gods before Me. You shall not make for yourself an idol, or any likeness of what is in heaven above or on the earth beneath or in the water under the earth." Exodus 20:3–4

PRAYER

Oh God, it is so hard not to focus on my signs of aging. When I am not pleased with what I see in the mirror, may I remember that You are more concerned with what You see in my heart. Help me to accept the changes that are happening to my hair as "the splendor of the old" and a crown of glory (Prov. 20:29 NIV).

You have said that charm is deceptive and beauty is vain. Your desire for me is to fear You, respect You, and put You first. I realize that when I focus more on my appearance than on developing a relationship with You, I am making my physical appearance an idol. Forgive me. In Jesus' name, *amen*.

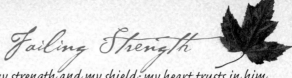

Failing Strength

The Lord is my strength and my shield; my heart trusts in him,
and I am helped. Psalm 28:7 (NIV)

The Lord is the everlasting God. . . . He gives strength to the weary
and increases the power of the weak . . . ; but those who hope in the Lord
will renew their strength. Isaiah 40:28–29, 31 (NIV)

I love you, O Lord, my strength. The Lord is my rock, my fortress
and my deliverer; my God is my rock, in whom I take refuge.
Psalm 18:1–2 (NIV)

My flesh and my heart may fail, but God is the strength of my heart
and my portion forever. Psalm 73:26 (NIV)

"For the joy of the Lord is your strength." Nehemiah 8:10b (NIV)

~

PRAYER

Father, these days I seem to have so little vim, vigor, and vitality. I
am looking to You for the strength I need. You have promised to give
strength to the weary and an increase of power to the weak. You have
said that those who hope in You will renew their strength. I love You,
oh Lord, my strength. I take refuge in You today. You are my portion
forever. I pray that the joy of the Lord will be my strength all day
long. In Jesus' name, *amen*.

The Lord is my strength and my shield;
my heart trusts in him, and I am helped.

*For he will command his angels
concerning you to guard you
in all your ways.*

Flourishing Fears

*The LORD is my light and my salvation; whom shall I fear?
The LORD is the defense of my life; whom shall I dread? Psalm 27:1*

*"The LORD is the one who goes ahead of you; He will be with you.
He will not fail you or forsake you. Do not fear or be dismayed."
Deuteronomy 31:8*

*For God has not given us a spirit of fear, but of power and of love
and of a sound mind. 2 Timothy 1:7 (NKJV)*

*Be anxious for nothing, but in everything by prayer and supplication
with thanksgiving let your requests be made known to God.
And the peace of God, which surpasses all comprehension, will
guard your hearts and your minds in Christ Jesus. Philippians 4:6–7*

*And pray that we may be delivered from wicked and evil men, for not
everyone has faith. But the Lord is faithful, and he will strengthen
and protect you from the evil one. 2 Thessalonians 3:2–3 (NIV)*

*For he will command his angels concerning you to guard you
in all your ways. Psalm 91:11–12 (NIV)*

*He will not fear evil tidings;
His heart is steadfast, trusting in the LORD. Psalm 112:7*

PRAYER

Oh Lord, You are my light, my salvation, and my defense. You have not given me a spirit of fear but a spirit of power, and love, and a sound mind. I know that I am not to be fearful or anxious about anything; but at this stage of my life there are so many uncertainties and unknowns. I am fearful of _____. I now commit my concerns to You, thanking You that You will give me peace.

Please protect me today from the evil one and evil men. Please command Your angels to guard me as I come and go. Help me to remember that no matter what I encounter, You have gone before me. You will always be with me. You will never fail me or forsake me! Help me to have a steadfast heart that trusts in You all day long. In Jesus' name, *amen.*

Being a Godly Example to the End

The righteous will flourish like a palm tree, they will grow like a cedar of Lebanon; planted in the house of the LORD, they will flourish in the courts of our God. They will still bear fruit in old age, they will stay fresh and green. Psalm 92:12–14 (NIV)

The steps of a man are established by the LORD; And He delights in his way. When he falls, he will not be hurled headlong, because the LORD is the One who holds his hand. I have been young and now I am old, yet I have not seen the righteous forsaken. Psalm 37:23–25

He will keep you strong to the end. 1 Corinthians 1:8a (NIV)

*In the same way, older women are to be reverent in behavior,
not slanderers, not addicted to much wine.
They are to teach what is good,
so that they may encourage the young women
to love their husbands and children. Titus 2:3–4 (HCSB)*

*So teach us to number our days,
That we may present to You a heart of wisdom. Psalm 90:12*

*O Lord GOD of hosts; do not let those who seek you
be dishonored because of me. Psalm 69:6b (NRSV)*

See also Psalm 78:4b–7; Mark 14:38 (NLT); Psalm 71:18; Romans 14:13b, 22

~

PRAYER

Oh great and awesome God, I praise You, because You promised to give the righteous a fruitful life, even in the senior years. You hold my hand and will not forsake me. My steps are established by You. Oh, how wonderful to know that You can enable me to stay fresh and green spiritually, even when physically I may be older and graying.

I know, as an older woman, You have given me the responsibility of teaching the younger women. May I never forget that before I can teach Your principles, I must model them in my life. I want to be reverent in my behavior, both in word and in deed. I desire to live and teach only what is good.

I know my days are numbered, dear Lord. I want to stay strong to the end. I do not want my words or actions to dishonor You. Help me to make the most of each day for Your glory. In the precious name of Jesus I pray, *amen.*

Dealing with Separation and Loss

Loss of a Loved One

God is our refuge and strength,
A very present help in trouble. Psalm 46:1

"Do not fear, for I [the LORD] have redeemed you;
I have called you by name; you are Mine!
When you pass through the waters, I will be with you;
And through the rivers, they will not overflow you." Isaiah 43:1b–2a

"Do not let your heart be troubled; believe in God, believe also in Me.
In My Father's house are many dwelling places; if it were not so,
I would have told you; for I go to prepare a place for you.
If I go and prepare a place for you, I will come again and receive you
to Myself, that where I am, there you may be also." John 14:1–3

Blessed be the God and Father of our Lord Jesus Christ,
the Father of mercies and God of all comfort,
who comforts us in all our affliction so that we will be able
to comfort those who are in any affliction with the comfort
with which we ourselves are comforted by God.
2 Corinthians 1:3–4

For He Himself has said, "I will never desert you, nor will I ever forsake you." Hebrews 13:5b

"My grace is sufficient for you, for my power is made perfect in weakness."
2 Corinthians 12:9 (NIV)

PRAYER

Oh God, You have said You will be our refuge and strength—a very present help in times of trouble. I need You to be that for me today. This loss is so overwhelming; I find it almost too much to bear. I am so thankful today that You are the God of all comfort who comforts us in all our tribulation. May I feel Your comforting hand upon me today. I know that You will use this tragedy in my life in the future to comfort others, but my heart is so troubled. I can only focus on today.

As I pass through these deep waters, You have told me that You will be with me—these waters will not overflow me. I am looking to You for the grace I need to make it through this time. I have so little strength. May Your power be demonstrated in my weakness. Help me to remember that wonderful promise You gave: "I will never desert you, nor will I ever forsake you."

I do believe in Your Son, Jesus Christ. I believe He is in heaven preparing a place for me. What a comfort it is to know that someday I, too, shall be in heaven. In Jesus' name, *amen.*

For He Himself has said,
"I will never desert you,
nor will I ever forsake you."

The Empty Nest

(*Sarah*) The quiet in our house was deafening. No incessant ringing of the telephone. No one coming through the door calling "Mom." No more emergency shopping trips to purchase necessities for tomorrow's project. No need to stay awake until the kids got home from a date or school event. Slowly it began to dawn on me: our kids had both gone off to college. Our nest was empty!

Whether I was ready or not, the time had come for our children to try their wings. They could not stay in our nest forever. My role as a mother had changed. I must begin the process of letting them go.

It didn't take long for me to discover how difficult this process would be. "Letting go" of my children meant letting go of my plans, and many times, my opinions. It meant letting go of my "right" to know what they were doing and what was happening in their lives. I found that I could not "let go" all at once. It was a process that would develop gradually as God revealed to me each area in which I needed to quit holding on.

Not many years later, however, I made another discovery—a wonderful one: when you really "let go" of your children, they will come back to you—not relating in the same way as before but in new and special ways. This new relationship of adult to adult will be so precious, as you see your children growing up and assuming responsibilities, as you see them put into practice those many things they learned "at Mother's knee."

Your adult children still need your love, your support, your counsel, and your prayers. You are and always will be their mother. And someday, if God wills, you will enter that marvelous season of life in which you will become a grandmother—a double blessing for mothers. You will thank God for the changing seasons of your life.

"The Lord is the One who goes ahead of you; He will be with you.
He will not fail you or forsake you. Do not fear or be dismayed."
Deuteronomy 31:8

PRAYER

Dear Father, I know that You have gone ahead of my children to this new location. You will be with them every moment. You will not fail them; nor will You forsake them. I pray that neither my children nor I will be fearful or dismayed. Please help me to trust You with their lives. In Jesus' name, *amen.*

Letting Go of My Children

In Their Marriages

"Haven't you read," He replied, "that He who created them in the beginning 'made them male and female,' and He also said: 'For this reason a man will leave his father and mother and be joined to his wife, and the two will become one flesh'?" Matthew 19:4–5 (HCSB)

~

PRAYER

Oh Father, please help me to "let go" of my daughter. I know she has "left" her father and me and has now been joined to her husband. But this is such a hard time for me. Help me to remember that this is Your plan for marriage. May I allow our children to establish their own home without interference from me. In Jesus' name, *amen.*

...a man will leave his father and mother and be joined to his wife ...

In Their Career Decisions

"The person who loves father or mother more than Me is not worthy of Me; the person who loves his son or daughter more than Me is not worthy of Me." Matthew 10:37 (HCSB)

~

PRAYER

Oh Father, this career decision my child has made is difficult for me. This was not the plan I had in mind for him. I know in my heart at this moment I love my child more than I love You. Forgive me. Change my heart. I desire to love You more than my child and release him into Your care. I truly want him to follow Your will. In Jesus' name, *amen.*

In Their Rebellion

Read the story of the prodigal son in Luke 15:11–32.

For the anger of man does not achieve the righteousness of God.
James 1:20

Turn to me, and be gracious to me;
Oh grant Your strength to Your servant,
And save the son of Your handmaid. Psalm 86:16

PRAYER

Father, like the son in the parable of the prodigal son, my child is rebelling. We have tried to train him in the way he should go, but he has turned his back on our teachings and has gone his own way. Please give me Your wisdom to know how to "let my child go to the far country." I need to let him experience the consequences of his sin. Help me to know when I am interfering or trying to rescue him.

Oh Lord, please save my son from destruction. Please draw him back to Yourself. Help me to remember that venting my anger will not produce righteousness in him. Soften my heart to know when he has truly repented. Just as You always receive me with great joy when I run back to You, so I desire to open my arms wide to receive him.

In this difficult time of waiting, I ask that You turn to me, pouring out Your grace and strength upon me. I want to trust You in this situation. Please help me, oh Lord. In Jesus' name, *amen*.

For the anger of man does not achieve the righteousness of God.

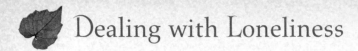# Dealing with Loneliness

Yet I am always with you; you hold me by my right hand. . . .
My flesh and my heart may fail, but God is the strength of my heart
and my portion forever. Psalm 73:23, 26 (NIV)

The LORD is faithful to all his promises and loving toward all he has made.
The LORD upholds all those who fall and lifts up all who are bowed down. . . .
You open your hand and satisfy the desires of every living thing.
The LORD is righteous in all his ways and loving toward all he has made.
The LORD is near to all who call on him, to all who call on him in truth.
He fulfills the desires of those who fear him; he hears their cry and saves them.
The LORD watches over all who love him.
Psalm 145:13b–14, 16–20a (NIV)

In Your presence is fullness of joy;
In Your right hand there are pleasures forever. Psalm 16:11b

PRAYER

Oh Father, I feel so lonely today. Help me not to depend on my feelings but on the facts of Your precious Word. Your Word tells me that You are faithful to all Your promises and loving toward all You have made. Because You love me, You have promised to be with me always—to hold me by the hand. You have also promised to lift up all who are bowed down. I call on You to lift me up today. Thank You for hearing my cry. I look to You to satisfy my desires in the way You think best.

You have said that "in Your presence is fullness of joy; in Your right hand there are pleasures forever." As I spend time in Your presence today, may I find that fullness of joy for my life. In Jesus' name, *amen.*

Becoming a Caregiver

I have set the LORD continually before me;
Because He is at my right hand, I will not be shaken. Psalm 16:8

Wisdom and knowledge will be the stability of your times.
Isaiah 33:6 (NKJV)

Now if any of you lacks wisdom, he should ask God, who gives to all
generously and without criticizing, and it will be given to him.
James 1:5 (HCSB)

I can do all things through Christ who strengthens me.
Philippians 4:13 (NKJV)

God has not given us a spirit of fearfulness,
but one of power, love, and sound judgment. 2 Timothy 1:7 (HCSB)

~

PRAYER

Oh dear Father, I find myself in the position of caregiver for
_____. What an awesome responsibility! I am apprehensive
about what the future may hold. But You, oh God, have not given
me a spirit of fear. Rather, You have given me power, love, and the
sound mind I need to handle this job. Help me to remember that
because You are at my right hand, You will keep me from being shaken.
Help me to remember that it is Your wisdom and knowledge that will
give me the stability I need. May I continually look to You for wisdom.
I ask You for the strength I need to deal with this difficult situation
today. (*Lay before God the particulars of your situation at this time.*) In
Jesus' name, *amen.*

Practical Tip

Ask God to bring to mind someone who is going through a changing season. Seek to minister to this person in a special way. If a person is lonely, invite her to a Bible study, a luncheon, or a fellowship. If a friend has lost a loved one, make a call or visit, or send her a card. Perhaps you have a friend who is a caregiver. Taking her place for an hour or two would be a welcomed "gift." Visits to a nursing home are always appreciated. God will show you just what to do, as you seek His wisdom. And don't be surprised if you receive the greatest blessing!

Garden Tip

Bare-root rosebushes will start faster if first soaked in water containing willow branches. Soak the willow branches for one day in water. Then soak the rosebushes overnight in the willow water.

CHAPTER TEN

Planting Seeds for the Harvest

Expanding My World

I have come to believe that you do not live in your house because
you like the shutters. . . . Think kingdom for a moment. Think circle
of influence. What does God desire to do through the flow of His love
in your life—to meet needs in your neighborhood or office that
would have the possibility of drawing someone to Himself?

— Esther Burroughs, Splash the Living Water

Wherever we are, we are to be witnesses of God's love. He provides many opportunities for us to communicate the gospel in our
homes, neighborhoods, and even throughout the world. When our
lives are bathed in prayer, we'll be ready to open our hearts and
homes to others whenever or wherever the Spirit leads us.

And He said to them, "Go into all the world and preach the gospel to all creation." Mark 16:15

"Go therefore and make disciples of all the nations, . . . and lo, I am with you always, even to the end of the age." Matthew 28:19a, 20b

Then He said to His disciples, "The harvest is abundant, but the workers are few. Therefore, pray to the Lord of the harvest to send out workers into His harvest." Matthew 9:37–38 (HCSB)

Devote yourselves to prayer; stay alert in it with thanksgiving. At the same time, pray also for us that God may open a door to us for the message, to speak the mystery of the Messiah . . . so that I may reveal it as I am required to speak. . . . Your speech should always be gracious, seasoned with salt, so that you may know how you should answer each person. Colossians 4:2–4, 6 (HCSB)

~

DAILY PRAYER

Oh Father, You have commanded us to go into all the world and present the gospel. You have asked us to pray for workers who will plant seeds for Your harvest. I do pray today that more workers will answer yes to Your call.

I know You have called me for this purpose also. Therefore, today I commit (anew or for the first time) to spreading the gospel. I ask that You open a door for me to proclaim Your message. I am willing to go wherever You send me. When that door opens, may I present the message of the gospel clearly. Help me to make certain that my speech is always gracious, seasoned with salt. I want to know how to answer each person I encounter.

Thank You that I can go into my world with the confidence that the same Lord who said, "Go," also said, "Lo, I am with you always." In Jesus' name, *amen*.

Being Obedient to Scatter Gospel Seeds

(*Sarah*) As a young stay-at-home mom with two preschoolers, my opportunities to "plant seeds for the harvest" seemed very limited. One day my Bible study teacher, Mary Ann Frazier, challenged us young mothers to share Jesus with everyone who came to our homes—from the repairman to the delivery person. I accepted her challenge and soon found many new opportunities to witness.

One morning as I looked out my den window, I saw five men building a brick wall around an area of our backyard. Immediately I felt apprehensive.

"Surely, Lord," I entreated, "You don't want me to go out and witness to five men! What will I say?"

I knew, however, that I had made a commitment to my heavenly Father. I must be obedient.

All morning I prayed for wisdom and courage. During the workers' lunch break, I ventured outside. But as I attempted to share the love of Jesus with them, my words got all tangled up. My presentation was not what I had planned. I quickly handed each man a copy of the New Testament and hurried back into the house, falling to my knees.

"Oh, Father," I cried. "I am so sorry! I really 'blew it.' I so wanted to present the gospel clearly. Please forgive me. I will try to do better next time."

Nineteen years later God brought the wife of one of those brick-layers into my life. Imagine my surprise at what she shared with me.

"I know you don't remember this, Sarah," she said, "but nineteen years ago my husband was the foreman on a bricklaying job in your backyard."

"Oh, yes, I do remember," I told her. That was an experience I would never forget.

She went on to say: "At that time my husband was not a Christian. He came home that night and told me about your sharing with him and his men. He had been a brickmason for twenty-two years and no one had ever before shared Jesus with him on his job. You planted a seed in his heart that day. He could never get over the fact that you came out into your carport and witnessed to all those men. That seed bore fruit nineteen years later when he received Jesus Christ as his Savior at age fifty-eight, five months before he died of cancer. I had been praying for him to become a Christian for thirty-eight years."

What valuable lessons I learned from this experience! God is not as interested in my ability as He is in my availability. It is not my oratory but my obedience that matters. My gospel presentation to those men was not perfect, but God's Word is. As I obediently "plant" the seeds of the gospel, they will bring forth fruit for the Master.

Planting Seeds
in and around My Home

We believe strongly that the place where God plants us is our mission field. All through the years we have sought to open our homes and hearts to those whom God brings into our lives. Today as never before, the world is at our doorsteps. We must be willing to be "open for business."

Opening My Home to Spread the Gospel

"And you shall be witnesses to Me in Jerusalem, and in all Judea and Samaria, and to the end of the earth." Acts 1:8 (NKJV)

And pray for us, too, that God may open a door for our message, so that we may proclaim the mystery of Christ . . . Be wise in the way you act toward outsiders; make the most of every opportunity.
Colossians 4:3, 5 (NIV)

Be wise in the way you act toward outsiders; make the most of every opportunity.

PRAYER

Oh Father, I want to be a witness—planting seeds for the harvest—wherever I may go. Help me to realize that I must first begin in and around my home—in my Jerusalem. As I stand at my front door, looking up and down my street, inspire me in ways I can be an effective witness in my neighborhood. I want to be wise in the way I act toward my neighbors and make the most of every opportunity. May I be willing to use my home as a tool for evangelizing my Jerusalem, if that is what You lead me to do. Please open doors for me to share the love of Jesus with my life and with my lips. In Jesus' name I pray, *amen.*

Opening My Home to Serve Others

"Oh that You would bless me indeed and enlarge my border, and that Your hand might be with me, and that You would keep me from harm that it may not pain me!" 1 Chronicles 4:10

If anyone serves, his service should be from the strength God provides, so that in everything God may be glorified through Jesus Christ.
1 Peter 4:11b (HCSB)

PRAYER

Oh Father, I want to be a blessing to those in my sphere of influence. Please expand my ministry as You desire. In this expansion I ask that Your hand be with me every step of the way. Please keep me from harm. I want to glorify You and You alone. I am looking to You for the empowerment to fulfill Your purposes through this ministry. In Jesus' name, *amen.*

Planting Seeds
Wherever God Leads Me

Finally, brethren, pray for us that the word of the Lord will spread rapidly and be glorified, just as it did also with you. 2 Thessalonians 3:1

Pray also for me, that whenever I open my mouth, words may be given me so that I will fearlessly make known the mystery of the gospel, for which I am an ambassador in chains. Pray that I may declare it fearlessly, as I should. Ephesians 6:19–20 (NIV)

To open their eyes so that they may turn from darkness to light and from the dominion of Satan to God, that they may receive forgiveness of sins and an inheritance among those who have been sanctified by faith in Me. Acts 26:18

Not that we are competent in ourselves to claim anything for ourselves, but our competence comes from God. 2 Corinthians 3:5 (NIV)

*Look to the LORD and his strength; seek his face always.
1 Chronicles 16:11 (NIV)*

~

PRAYER

Dear Father, I pray that as I follow Your leading, the Word of the Lord will spread rapidly. Whenever I open my mouth, I ask You to give me the words to speak. May I speak boldly and fearlessly, as I should. May those to whom I speak have their eyes opened, so that they will turn from darkness to light and receive that eternal inheritance You long for them to have. I know that my competency comes from You and You alone. I will look to You for the strength I need. In Jesus' name, *amen.*

Practical Tip

OPEN YOUR HOME IN MINISTRY TO OTHERS

1. Bring *help:*
   - To ministers, missionaries, and other Christian workers
   - To those who are in need of counsel and guidance
   - To newcomers in your church or community
   - To your own family
     (by inviting them to your home for a meal, for tea,
     for a fellowship, or as overnight guests)

2. Bring *healing:*
   - To those in need of healing—physically, mentally, emotionally,
   or spiritually (by counseling or caring for them in your home)

3. Bring *happiness:*
   - To all those who are recipients of your hospitality
     (by hosting teas, parties, and fellowships in your home)

4. Bring *hope:*
   - To a world without hope
     (by opening your home for evangelistic coffees, Bible
     studies, birthday parties for Jesus, other special events)

Garden Tip

Chrysanthemums want to bloom early in June. To prevent this, cut
or trim all the buds until July 4. Then your plants will produce lovely
fall blossoms.

CHAPTER ELEVEN

It's Springtime in My Garden

New Beginnings

The Master Gardener specializes in new beginnings!
—Karla Dornacher, *Down a Garden Path*

~

Jesus Christ brings about a new beginning when He comes into our lives as Savior and Lord. Also, He initiates a fresh start when our relationships with Him need to be revitalized. Even when we've experienced wintery times of suffering, change, or discouragement, we can still be assured that He will bring the springtime into our gardens!

Behold, I will do a new thing, Now it shall spring forth;
Shall you not know it? I will even make a road in the wilderness
And rivers in the desert. Isaiah 43:19 (NKJV)

You will be like a well-watered garden,
like a spring whose waters never fail. Isaiah 58:11b (NIV)

~

DAILY PRAYER

Father, I am asking You to do a new thing in my life. I pray that as this new thing springs forth, I will know it has come from You. I am looking to You, oh Lord, to make a road in my wilderness and rivers in my desert. I desire for my life to be like a watered garden, and like a spring whose waters never fail. In Jesus' name, *amen.*

A Transformation to Beauty

(*Sarah*) Several years ago my husband and I visited the beautiful Butchart Gardens in Victoria, Canada. We were surprised to learn that the magnificent Sunken Garden there was once a limestone quarry. As I gazed in amazement at the pictures of what the quarry had looked like in its original state, it was almost impossible to imagine that this transformation could have taken place. And yet, because of the vision and fortitude of one young woman, Jenny Butchart, the Butchart Gardens are a masterpiece for the world to enjoy.

What if Mrs. Butchart, looking down into that fifty-foot hole, had seen only a desolate pit strewn with rocks, dotted with puddles of dirty water? Instead, she visualized the garden it could become. Over a period of time, with ingenuity, exuberance, and much backbreaking work, this limestone quarry was transformed into a spectacular sunken garden. Her vision became a reality. Now, many years later, the entire landscape surrounding the quarry displays the most beautiful gardens in the world—the Butchart Gardens.

When God looked at us in our sinful condition, we must have been as unattractive as that quarry in Canada. In our sinful state we were colorless, lifeless, and desolate. But praise His name, because of His infinite love and mercy, He saw what we could become, when transformed by His grace. He knew us through and through because He made us. He knew that through the power of His Son Jesus Christ, we would become new creations. Thus God sent His beloved Son to die for our sins on the cross at Calvary. When we receive this new life in Christ, as we allow Him to do His work in us, we, too, can become fruitful gardens—springs in the desert to glorify Him forever.

When by His grace Patti and I were saved so many years ago, God began His transforming work on us. Today we know we are far from what He wants us to be; but praise God, He's not finished with us yet. As we reflect on these truths, we cannot do less than exalt His name continually. What amazing grace and love He has poured out on us! He has given us new life in Christ. Praise His holy name!

New Life in Christ

Those of us who have received new life in Christ should be continually praising God for the priceless gift of love made possible through His Son.

Praise be to the God and Father of our Lord Jesus Christ! In his great mercy he has given us new birth into a living hope through the resurrection of Jesus Christ from the dead. 1 Peter 1:3 (NIV)

But God proves His own love for us in that while we were still sinners Christ died for us! Romans 5:8 (HCSB)

In Him we have redemption through His blood, the forgiveness of our trespasses, according to the riches of His grace. Ephesians 1:7 (HCSB)

For by grace you are saved through faith, and this is not from yourselves; it is God's gift—not from works, so that no one can boast. Ephesians 2:8–9 (HCSB)

Therefore if anyone is in Christ, there is a new creation; old things have passed away, and look, new things have come. 2 Corinthians 5:17 (HCSB)

Therefore if anyone is in Christ, there is a new creation; old things have passed away, and look, new things have come.

P R A Y E R

Oh merciful God and Father of our Lord Jesus Christ, I bless Your holy name. Even though I was a sinner, because of Your great love for me, You sent Your only Son to die on the cross for my sins. You have given me a new birth into a living hope, through the resurrection of Your Son Jesus Christ.

I praise You that because of the riches of His grace, through the blood of Jesus, I have redemption, the forgiveness of sins. It is not because of my good works that I am now Your child; it was Your gift to me. Thank You, oh God, that I am a new creation in Christ. Old things have passed away. New things have come as a result. I give You praise this day for my eternal salvation. In Jesus' name I pray, *amen*.

A Fresh Start

Every Christian woman experiences a "winter" season at some point in her life. Sometimes it is a "desert" experience, a time of spiritual drought. No matter how dry your desert or severe your winter, God can enable you to make a fresh start. He will take your life and turn it into something beautiful. You can blossom and flourish once more.

Jesus has provided within you a spring of living water. He promised that "whoever drinks the water I give him will never thirst. Indeed, the water I give him will become in him a spring of water welling up to eternal life" (John 4:14, NIV). Through the power of the Holy Spirit you can be renewed, refreshed, and replenished so that "from [your] innermost being will flow rivers of living water" (John 7:38).

For lo, the winter is past, the rain is over and gone.
The flowers appear on the earth; the time of singing has come,
And the voice of the turtledove is heard in our land.
Song of Solomon 2:11–12 (NKJV)

May your roots go down deep into the soil of God's marvelous love.
Ephesians 3:17b (NLT)

"Forget the former things; do not dwell on the past.
See, I am doing a new thing! Now it springs up."
Isaiah 43:18–19 (NIV)

Trust in the LORD with all your heart
and lean not on your own understanding;
in all your ways acknowledge him,
and he will make your paths straight. Proverbs 3:5–6 (NIV)

Now may the God of hope fill you with all joy and peace in believing,
so that you may overflow with hope by the power of the Holy Spirit.
Romans 15:13 (HCSB)

But I trust in your unfailing love; my heart rejoices in your salvation.
I will sing to the LORD, for he has been good to me. Psalm 13:5 (NIV)

PRAYER

Lord, my "winter season" has been so difficult. Help me to realize that just as springtime follows winter, something new can spring forth in my life after my "winter season" is past. Because of You, there is hope for me. As I let my roots grow down deep into the soil of Your love, I will draw the nourishment necessary to have a fruitful life. Once more it can be springtime in my heart.

Help me to forget the former things—to stop dwelling on my past. May I realize that You will do new things in my life as I trust You with my future. As I acknowledge You in all my ways, You will make my paths straight. My hope is in You, Lord. You are the God of hope.

Please fill me with all joy and peace as I trust in the power of the Holy Spirit, so that I will overflow with hope. With this hope I shall look forward with great expectation to the new things you have planned for me. Once again I will be able to rejoice in my salvation and sing praises for Your goodness to me. In the precious name of Jesus I pray, *amen.*

Garden Tip

When you want huge daylily blooms for the next day, water well at sunset, and your flowers will be larger the next morning.

Applications

How to Receive New Life in Christ

Jesus Christ is the source of eternal life. He wants to provide new life for all. He said in John 14:6, "I am the way and the truth and the life. No one comes to the Father except through me" (NIV). If there has never been a time when you have repented of your sins and received Jesus Christ as your Savior and Lord, please use this moment to do so. You may pray a prayer like this as you ask Jesus to come into your heart:

Dear Jesus,

I acknowledge that I am a sinner in need of a Savior. I believe that You died on the cross for my sins. Please forgive me of my sins. I now turn from my sins and put my faith in You. I ask You, Lord Jesus, to come into my heart as my Savior and Lord. Thank You for giving me eternal life. In Your name I pray, amen.

~

These things I have written to you who believe in the name of the Son of God, that you may know that you have eternal life.
1 John 5:13 (NKJV)

How to Experience Spiritual Renewal

If you are a believer but have been experiencing a "winter" season, God wants to do a new thing in your life, starting today. He wants to make you into a "watered garden, . . . whose springs do not fail" (Isa. 58:11).

The following action plan will lead you to the "springtime"—to a fresh start—in your life.

We suggest the following steps:

1. Confess and forsake your sin (1 John 1:9).
2. Surrender to God's full control (Rom. 12:1–2).
3. Commit to a life of trust in God and obedience to His commands (Prov. 3:5–6).

~

What a joy it has been to share our hearts with you! We pray that your prayer life has been enriched, your relationship to our Lord strengthened, and your knowledge of how to pray God's Word deepened. Please feel free to contact us through our publisher.

—*Sarah Maddox and Patti Webb*

Endnotes

INTRODUCTION

1. Susan L. Lenzkes, "A Morning Prayer," *A Silver Pen for Cloudy Days* (Grand Rapids, Mich.: Zondervan, 1987), 6.

2. Elisabeth Elliot, *Let Me Be a Woman* (Wheaton, Ill.: Tyndale House, 1976), 52.

3. From "The Beautiful Garden of Prayer" by Eleanor Allen Schroll and J. H. Fillmore, cited in Sarah Maddox and Patti Webb, *A Mother's Garden of Prayer* (Nashville: Broadman & Holman, 1999), xi.

CHAPTER TWO

1. Avery T. Willis Jr., *MasterLife, Developing a Rich Personal Relationship with the Master* (Nashville: Broadman & Holman, 1998), 91. Comments in parentheses are from the authors.

CHAPTER SIX

1. Author unknown.

CHAPTER EIGHT

1. Sarah Maddox and Patti Webb, *A Mother's Garden of Prayer* (Nashville: Broadman & Holman, 1999).

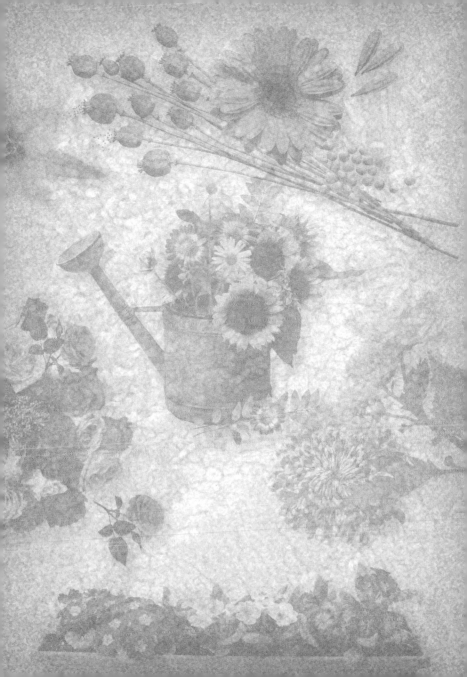